MY FINAL ANSWER

CELEBRITY EDITION

THIRTY INTERACTIVE QUIZZES
THAT PUT *YOU* IN THE HOT SEAT

JOHN HUDSON TINER

BARBOUR BOOKS
An Imprint of Barbour Publishing, Inc.

MY FINAL ANSWER

CELEBRITY EDITION

© 2002 by Barbour Publishing, Inc.

ISBN 1-58660-499-6

Published by Barbour Books, an imprint of Barbour Publishing, Inc.,
P.O. Box 719, Uhrichsville, Ohio 44683, www.barbourbooks.com

ecpa Member of the
Evangelical Christian
Publishers Association

Printed in the United States of America.
5 4 3 2

INTRODUCTION

Here's *My Final Answer—Celebrity Edition*, the long-awaited follow-up to the best-selling *My Final Answer*. Each of these 360 questions tests your knowledge of the Heroes of the Faith—missionaries, song and hymn writers, Bible characters, and others who dedicated their lives to the service of God. Each quiz has fun, interesting, and increasingly more difficult questions. Challenge yourself or use it in a group—the book lends itself well to a "quiz show" format, with a contestant and a moderator.

Each quiz features twelve levels of multiple-choice questions, beginning with easy material that is generally known. But the challenge increases as you advance through the levels. Answer the first four levels without a wrong answer, and you've won Bronze. If you can successfully navigate eight levels of questioning, you'll earn Silver. And if you survive all twelve levels without a miss, you'll win Gold! Be forewarned—to be successful you'll need to know a wide range of information.

But you will have help. In each quiz, you get three Bonuses: Use them carefully (in combination with your knowledge) and you can win! Once in each quiz, you can:

DOUBLE YOUR CHANCES (beginning on page 193): Look up this bonus to learn two of the wrong answers.

HAVE A HINT (beginning on page 205): Look up this bonus for some extra information—it may be a word play or some reference to the popular culture— to give you a clue to the correct answer.

LOOK IN THE BOOK (beginning on page 229): Look up this bonus for a Bible reference that contains a key word from the correct answer. Unless otherwise identified, the key words come from passages in the New International Version of the Bible.

You have three Bonuses (one of each type) in each twelve-question quiz. All Bonuses, like the answers, are listed by level rather than quiz, so that you don't inadvertently see information on the next question as you're checking your current one.

The ANSWER section begins on page 241.

Are you ready for the challenge? Step up to the "hot seat" and show your knowledge about those who through the ages have lived for Jesus! As you prove how much you know, remember Hebrews 11:39: "These were all commended for their faith." That's what *My Final Answer—Celebrity Edition* is all about!

QUIZZES

THIRTY INTERACTIVE QUIZZES THAT PUT YOU IN THE HOT SEAT

TRIVIA FOR LIFE

QUIZ 1

What was the first major publication from Johannes Gutenberg's printing press?

    a) *Poor Richard's Almanack*
    b) Saint Augustine's book *The City of God*
    c) the entire Bible
    d) the Dead Sea Scrolls

Page 193   Page 205   Page 229   Page 241

LEVEL 2

What letters did Joni Eareckson Tada use to sign her first paintings?

a) GIG for "God Is Good"
b) PTL for "Praise the Lord"
c) WWJD for "What Would Jesus Do?"
d) JAF for "Joni and Friends"

LEVEL 3

In addition to Genesis, what other book of the Bible starts, "In the beginning"?

a) Job   c) Luke
b) Daniel   d) John

BRONZE

The phrase "Come, we that love the Lord" is from what song by Isaac Watts?

a) "I'm Not Ashamed to Own My Lord"
b) "Sing the Mighty Power of God"
c) "We're Marching to Zion"
d) "There Is a Land of Pure Delight"

Pages 194–196   Pages 207–212   Pages 230–232   Pages 242–244

LEVEL 5

What was the blind man doing when he called to Jesus on the road outside Jericho?
    a) begging
    b) weaving fabric
    c) resting
    d) making pottery

LEVEL 6

To escape from Herod, where did Joseph and Mary take Baby Jesus?
    a) Ethiopia   c) Tyre
    b) Rome   d) Egypt

LEVEL 7

Which would best describe Dwight L. Moody's approach to his ministry?
    a) conservative and personal Christianity
    b) higher criticism of the Bible
    c) promoting unity among Christian
        denominations
    d) speaking effectively for the Social Gospel
        movement

Pages 197–199   Pages 213–218   Pages 233–235   Pages 245–247

SILVER

Which of the following works is by the artist Albrecht Dürer?

   a) *Hands of the Apostle,*
      better known as "praying hands"
   b) *The Adoration of the Magi*
   c) *Madonna and Child with the Infant St. John*
   d) *Pietà* in St. Peter's Basilica

LEVEL 9

What job did Rachel do?

   a) shepherdess   c) groomed horses
   b) seamstress   d) hired servant

LEVEL 10

George Macdonald, who influenced C. S. Lewis, wrote what children's book?

   a) *At the Back of the North Wind*
   b) *The Natural History of a Candle*
   c) *The Swiss Family Robinson*
   d) *The Secret Garden*

Pages 200–202   Pages 219–224   Pages 236–238   Pages 248–250

LEVEL 11

How many years older was Aaron than Moses?
- a) three years
- b) twenty years
- c) twelve years
- d) none, they were twins

GOLD

Who was the person who first wrapped Jesus' crucified body in about seventy-five pounds of myrrh and aloes?
- a) Nicodemus
- b) Joanna
- c) Mary Magdalene and the "other" Mary
- d) Martha

THIRTY INTERACTIVE QUIZZES THAT PUT YOU IN THE HOT SEAT

TRIVIA
FOR
LIFE

QUIZ 2

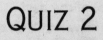

In the motto of his abolitionist paper, who did Frederick Douglass say was "father of us all"?

   a) God
   b) invention
   c) truth
   d) poverty

Page 193   Page 205   Page 229   Page 241

LEVEL 2

How did Mary describe herself to the angel who announced she would give birth to Jesus?

- a) "[The Lord] has shown his favor and taken away my disgrace."
- b) "I am the Lord's servant."
- c) "Why is this happening to me?"
- d) "I am worn out and my master is old."

LEVEL 3

In his song, what time of day does Charles Austin Miles enter "In the Garden"?

- a) "in the cool of the day"
- b) "while the dew is still on the roses"
- c) "though the night around me is falling"
- d) "at three in the afternoon"

BRONZE

What was Cain's reply when God asked him about his brother?

- a) "Here am I."
- b) "Am I my brother's keeper?"
- c) "Am I in the place of God?"
- d) "What wrong am I guilty of?"

Pages 194–196   Pages 207–212   Pages 230–232   Pages 242–244

LEVEL 5

What was the profession of Lew Wallace, the author of *Ben Hur*?

a) scientist   c) missionary

b) explorer   d) military leader

LEVEL 6

Complete this quotation by George Washington Carver: "It is service to others that measures..."?

a) "success."

b) "heavenly compensation."

c) "genius."

d) "achieved dreams."

LEVEL 7

How is Tabitha described in the Bible?

a) as carrying gossip and sowing strife

b) as the first Christian in Europe

c) as a woman who had been sick for twelve years

d) as doing good and helping the poor

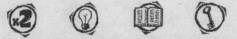

Pages 197–199 Pages 213–218 Pages 233–235 Pages 245–247

SILVER

What type of water is described in "Jesus, Keep Me Near the Cross" by Fanny J. Crosby?

   a) "an ocean deep"   c) "rain for a thirsty land"
   b) "a healing stream" d) "cool, melting snow"

LEVEL 9

What was George Whitefield's greatest strength as a preacher?

   a) his dignified presentation
   b) his scholarship
   c) his profound theological ideas
   d) his dramatic speaking style

LEVEL 10

How did Jesus reply when Martha said, "If you had been here my brother would not have died"?

   a) "Your brother will rise again."
   b) "Don't be alarmed. He's alive!"
   c) "One who lives for pleasure is dead even while alive."
   d) "The body without the spirit is dead."

Pages 200–202 Pages 219–224 Pages 236–238 Pages 248–250

LEVEL 11

Who first encouraged George Whitefield to visit the United States and preach there?
   a) Benjamin Franklin
   b) John and Charles Wesley
   c) Jonathan Edwards
   d) Oliver Cromwell

GOLD

What was the title of Mahalia Jackson's first major successful song recording?
   a) "God Gonna Separate the Wheat from the Tares"
   b) "I'm Going to Move On Up a Little Higher"
   c) "Precious Lord, Hold My Hand"
   d) "Abraham, Martin, and John"

Pages 203–204   Pages 225–228   Pages 239–240   Pages 251–252

THIRTY INTERACTIVE QUIZZES THAT PUT YOU IN THE HOT SEAT

TRIVIA
FOR
LIFE

QUIZ 3

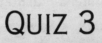

What is one of the principles that Martin Luther believed about Christianity?

a) A believer is justified by his or her works.

b) Christians have direct access to God.

c) Christians should be guided by law, Gospel, and Church heritage.

d) Believers could receive revelation through dreams.

Page 193   Page 205   Page 229   Page 241

Clara Barton was the founder of what organization?
- a) YMCA
- b) Salvation Army
- c) The Sanitary Commission
- d) American Red Cross

LEVEL 3

Who is the artist of *Creation of Adam* in the Sistine Chapel?
- a) Michelangelo
- b) Albrecht Dürer
- c) Leonardo da Vinci
- d) Roger Tory Peterson

BRONZE

What does Mary Magdalene have to do with the number seven?
- a) She kept watch at the tomb of Jesus for seven days.
- b) She had seven demons driven from her.
- c) Jesus told her to forgive seven times seventy.
- d) She provided seven loaves to feed the multitude.

Pages 194–196 Pages 207–212 Pages 230–232 Pages 242–244

LEVEL 5

Where does Julia Ward Howe say that Jesus was born in her song "Battle Hymn of the Republic"?
- a) in a papyrus basket
- b) in the beauty of the lilies
- c) in a manger
- d) as a rose of Sharon

LEVEL 6

How were Esther and Mordecai related?
- a) husband and wife
- b) brother and sister
- c) cousins
- d) father and daughter

LEVEL 7

What title could be used to describe Charles Spurgeon?
- a) Missionary Exemplar
- b) Great Orator
- c) abolitionist and reformer
- d) Father of English Protestantism

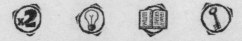

Pages 197–199   Pages 213–218   Pages 233–235   Pages 245–247

Why did Joseph of the Old Testament go to Egypt?

    a) He was sold as a slave into Egypt.
    b) His parents took him to Egypt to avoid those who sought to kill him.
    c) He went into Egypt to tell Pharaoh to release his people.
    d) He went into Egypt in his old age because of a famine.

In addition to abolition of slavery, what other cause did Sojourner Truth champion?

    a) retirement benefits for Civil War veterans
    b) women's rights
    c) nursing and hospital reform
    d) child welfare

LEVEL 10

What book did Dietrich Bonhoeffer finish while in a German prison?
- a) *The Cost of Discipleship*
- b) *A Testament from Prison*
- c) *The Sacrifice from Cell 92*
- d) *Principles of a Pacifist*

LEVEL 11

To whom did Priscilla and her husband explain the way of God more adequately?
- a) Demetrius
- b) Barnabas
- c) Lydia
- d) Apollos

GOLD

What was one of Amy Carmichael's primary activities?
- a) rescuing girls who had been dedicated to pagan temples
- b) protecting the intellectual property of songwriters
- c) prohibiting the sale of alcohol
- d) abolishing slavery

Pages 203–204   Pages 223–228   Pages 238–240   Pages 250–252

THIRTY INTERACTIVE QUIZZES THAT PUT YOU IN THE HOT SEAT

TRIVIA
FOR
LIFE

QUIZ 4

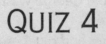

LEVEL 1

The William and Gloria Gaither song "There's Something about That Name" refers to what specific name?

    a) Jesus
    b) Lion of Judah
    c) The Family of God
    d) Gentle Shepherd

Page 193

Page 205

Page 229

Page 241

LEVEL 2

What did Aaron do for his brother Moses?
- a) remained in Midian to care for Moses' flocks
- b) was the orator for the words of Moses
- c) laid his hands on Joshua as a replacement for Moses
- d) disputed with the archangel Michael about the body of Moses

LEVEL 3

For what crops did George Washington Carver develop new uses?
- a) strawberries and blueberries
- b) cotton and flax
- c) corn and rice
- d) peanuts and sweet potatoes

BRONZE

In the refrain of "There Is Power in the Blood," how does Lewis Ellis Jones describe the power?
- a) "cleansing"   c) "purer"
- b) "wonder working"   d) "everlasting"

LEVEL 5

Who did John the Baptist call a brood of vipers?
- a) the apostles of Jesus
- b) the Roman authorities
- c) the Pharisees and Sadducees
- d) the people of Nazareth

LEVEL 6

In his song, what does Charles Wesley desire in order to sing "My great Redeemer's praise"?
- a) "a golden voice"
- b) "a mountaintop"
- c) "majestic words"
- d) "a thousand tongues"

LEVEL 7

Why did Frederick Bailey take the name Frederick Douglass?
- a) to conceal his shame at being the son of a white slaveholder
- b) to bring honor to the man who helped him escape
- c) to restore his true name from the one given him by his slave master
- d) to make it more difficult to be traced as a runaway slave

Pages 197–199 Pages 213–218 Pages 233–235 Pages 245–247

How many of Eve's sons are named in the Bible?
- a) none
- b) two
- c) three
- d) seven

What was Rebekah doing when the servant came to find a wife for Isaac?
- a) bringing garments to be washed
- b) driving cattle to pasture
- c) carrying a jar for water
- d) gathering firewood

What period of time is *not* mentioned in the song "Amazing Grace" by John Newton?
- a) days
- b) month
- c) hour
- d) ten thousand years

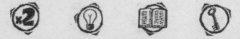

Pages 200–202   Pages 219–224   Pages 236–238   Pages 248–250

LEVEL 11

Which statement is true about R. G. LeTourneau?
- a) He gave up a promising business career to become a missionary.
- b) He began a publishing firm to provide missionary material in the French language.
- c) He sold his companies rather than build weapons of war.
- d) He was an industrialist who tithed 90 percent of his income.

GOLD

What was Eric Liddell's nickname?
- a) Galloping Ghost
- b) Little Magician
- c) Lost Dutchman
- d) Flying Scotsman

Pages 203–204   Pages 225–228   Pages 239–240   Pages 251–252

THIRTY INTERACTIVE QUIZZES THAT PUT YOU IN THE HOT SEAT

TRIVIA
FOR
LIFE

QUIZ 5

LEVEL 1

How did the father of John the Baptist communicate the name of his son to his relatives?

   a) He wrote on a tablet.

   b) He whispered to his wife.

   c) He pointed to a prophecy in Scripture.

   d) He wrote in the sand.

Page 193   Page 205   Page 229   Page 241

LEVEL 2

Billy Graham's preaching tours are known by what name?

a) campaigns   c) crusades
b) rallies   d) gospel meetings

LEVEL 3

What employment did Dwight L. Moody leave to begin his religious activity?

a) train conductor
b) postal employee
c) shoe salesman
d) baseball player

BRONZE

From what was Eve's first covering made?

a) garments of skin
b) woven flax and barley straw
c) fig leaves
d) knitted material of linen and wool

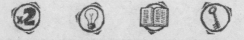

LEVEL 5

Why did Eric Liddell miss the 1924 Olympic 100-meter race, his best event?

    a) He wanted Harold Abrahams to win.
    b) He was disqualified because he had been born in China.
    c) He missed the taxi taking him to the event.
    d) He chose not to run on Sunday.

LEVEL 6

Which of David's wives is mentioned in Matthew?

    a) Ahinoam   c) Uriah's wife (Bathsheba)
    b) Abigail   d) Michal

LEVEL 7

What follows the phrase "Rescue the perishing" in the refrain of the Fanny Crosby hymn of the same name?

    a) "throw out the lifeline"
    b) "pray for the harvest"
    c) "care for the dying"
    d) "look to the Savior"

Pages 197–199   Pages 213–218   Pages 233–235   Pages 245–247

After accepting the presidency of the College of New Jersey (later Princeton University), how did Jonathan Edwards die?

- a) from a smallpox inoculation
- b) at the hands of an angry mob
- c) while trying to rescue his wife from their burning home
- d) of a stroke while delivering an impassioned sermon

LEVEL 9

Who was Silas?

- a) a teacher of Priscilla and Aquila
- b) the father of Timothy
- c) Paul's traveling companion
- d) John the Baptist's chief disciple

Pages 200–201   Pages 219–222   Pages 236–237   Pages 248–249

LEVEL 10

How did Philip approach the chariot of the Ethiopian eunuch?
- a) while running
- b) while riding a camel
- c) being carried there in a whirlwind
- d) while waiting at an oasis

LEVEL 11

What did Mary Slessor do for the British in Calabar, Nigeria?
- a) select routes for trading in palm oil
- b) arbitrate disputes between native tribes
- c) spy on German activities during World War I
- d) explore the Zambezi River

GOLD

Whose scientific work did Jonathan Edwards read with great interest?
- a) Benjamin Franklin's
- b) Isaac Newton's
- c) Archimedes'
- d) Michael Faraday's

Pages 202–204 Pages 223–228 Pages 238–240 Pages 250–252

THIRTY INTERACTIVE QUIZZES THAT PUT YOU IN THE HOT SEAT

TRIVIA
FOR
LIFE

QUIZ 6

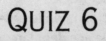

In Charlotte Elliott's song "Just as I Am," how many pleas did she have?

    a) not one
    b) one
    c) seven times seventy
    d) all

Page 193

Page 205

Page 229

Page 241

LEVEL 2

Henry Ward Beecher's sister Harriet was the author of what book?

   a) *John Brown's Body*
   b) *Poor Laws and Paupers*
   c) *Uncle Tom's Cabin*
   d) *Incidents in the Life of a Slave Girl*

LEVEL 3

What kind of accident caused Joni Eareckson Tada to be paralyzed?

   a) fall from her horse
   b) diving accident while swimming
   c) automobile accident late at night
   d) sports injury while playing lacrosse

BRONZE

Where was the mansion located in the Ira Stanphill song?

   a) just over the hilltop
   b) beside still waters
   c) in a valley below
   d) on level ground

Pages 194–196   Pages 207–212   Pages 230–232   Pages 242–244

LEVEL 5

The statement "Your people will be my people and your God my God" was made by Ruth to whom?

a) David
b) Boaz
c) Naomi
d) village elders

LEVEL 6

While Jesus visited Martha and her family at Bethany, what was true about the housework?

a) Martha left it undone to listen to Jesus.
b) Martha sent a servant girl to hire a room in which to serve Jesus.
c) Martha was distracted by it.
d) Neighbors helped Martha do the housework.

LEVEL 7

How did Paul escape from those who waited to kill him as he left Damascus?

a) through a tunnel
b) being let down from the wall in a basket
c) an angel blinded the eyes of his enemies
d) in the confusion of an earthquake

Pages 197–199   Pages 213–218   Pages 233–235   Pages 245–247

SILVER

Joseph Lister was a Christian and great surgeon who is credited with what medical discovery?

   a) vaccination against smallpox
   b) blood transfusion
   c) anesthesia
   d) antiseptic surgery

LEVEL 9

What action ensured that *My Utmost for His Highest* by Oswald Chambers was published?

   a) Robert Louis Stevenson gave a favorable review.
   b) Chambers wrote it while in quarantine.
   c) Charles Spurgeon rescued the manuscript from a trash container.
   d) Gertrude Hobbs, his wife, transcribed his lectures.

Pages 200–201   Pages 219–222   Pages 236–237   Pages 248–249

LEVEL 10

Which C. S. Lewis book is about his marriage late in life?
- a) *Till We Have Faces*
- b) *Allegory of Love*
- c) *Surprised by Joy*
- d) *Beyond Personality*

LEVEL 11

What was the religion of Watchman Nee's parents and grandparents?

a) Islam	c) Confucianism
b) Christianity	d) Buddhism

GOLD

What native custom did Mary Slessor battle in Africa?
- a) exposure of the elderly
- b) murder of twin babies
- c) poaching of elephants for their ivory
- d) blood rites to seal agreements

Pages 202–204   Pages 223–228   Pages 238–240   Pages 250–252

THIRTY INTERACTIVE QUIZZES THAT PUT YOU IN THE HOT SEAT

TRIVIA
FOR
LIFE

QUIZ 7

What was the hiding place referred to in Corrie ten Boom's book?
- a) a secret room
- b) a childhood nursery rhyme
- c) a tree house
- d) a shelter for battered women

Page 193

Page 205

Page 229

Page 241

After the Sabbath, what did Salome, Mary Magdalene, and Mary the mother of James take to the tomb of Jesus?

   a) spices
   b) burial linens
   c) olive branches and flowers
   d) marker of stones for His tomb

LEVEL 3

What United States holiday has its roots in a celebration Priscilla Mullins and her future husband, John Alden, attended when it was first held?

   a) Independence Day   c) Christmas
   b) Thanksgiving   d) Columbus Day

In what river did John the Baptist preach and baptize?

   a) Tigris   c) Jordan
   b) Pishon   d) Hebron

Pages 194–196 Pages 207–212 Pages 230–232 Pages 242–244

LEVEL 5

What did Jesus do for the widow who lived in the town of Nain?

    a) went to eat in her house
    b) granted her justice against her adversary
    c) healed her of a disease she had suffered
       for twelve years
    d) raised her only son from the dead

LEVEL 6

Why did Dante Alighieri write *The Divine Comedy* in Italian rather than Latin?

    a) He was forbidden to publish in Latin.
    b) He preferred to write in the language of
       the common people.
    c) Anything ancient repelled him.
    d) It was the only language he knew.

How was Corrie ten Boom released from Ravensbruck concentration camp?
- a) by a clerical error
- b) American soldiers liberated her
- c) through her death
- d) by a guard who had become a Christian

What book did Watchman Nee began writing at the age of twenty-three?
- a) *The Normal Christian Life*
- b) *The Spiritual Man*
- c) *Love Not the World*
- d) *A Living Sacrifice*

LEVEL 9

How long did Moses' mother hide him after he was born?
- a) three months
- c) twelve years
- b) seven weeks
- d) forty days

Pages 199–201   Pages 217–222   Pages 235–237   Pages 247–249

What name could be applied to Watchman Nee?
- a) Great Commoner
- b) Blind Evangelist
- c) Sportsman Christian
- d) Man of Suffering

Before devoting himself fully to religious matters, what did Blaise Pascal study with Pierre de Fermat?
- a) the orbits of planets
- b) the classification of plants
- c) the speed of falling bodies
- d) problems involving probability and statistics

GOLD

Rebekah received what kind of gifts from the servant sent to find a wife for Isaac?
- a) nose ring and bracelets
- b) honey, pistachio nuts, and almonds
- c) sweet cakes
- d) goats and sheep

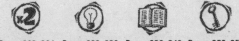

Pages 202–204   Pages 223–228   Pages 238–240   Pages 250–252

THIRTY INTERACTIVE QUIZZES THAT PUT YOU IN THE HOT SEAT

TRIVIA
FOR
LIFE

QUIZ 8

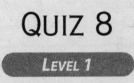

Why did God not let David build the temple (house of God)?
    a) Israel under David was too poor.
    b) David had become too old and weak.
    c) David had shed much blood.
    d) David could not unite warring tribes.

Page 193   Page 205   Page 229   Page 241

LEVEL 2

What is the title of the William and Gloria Gaither song that explains why "I can face tomorrow"?

    a) "Jesus, We Just Want to Thank You"
    b) "Because He Lives"
    c) "A Hill Called Mount Calvary"
    d) "His Name Is Life"

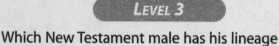

LEVEL 3

Which New Testament male has his lineage traced through Ruth?

    a) the Ethiopian
    b) Cornelius
    c) Saul (Paul)
    d) Joseph, the husband of Mary

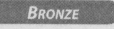

BRONZE

In Frances Havergal's song, what words come after "I gave My life for thee"?

    a) "with thorns upon My head"
    b) "My precious blood I shed"
    c) "come ye blessed"
    d) "I bring rich gifts to thee"

Pages 194–196   Pages 207–212 Pages 230–232 Pages 242–244

LEVEL 5

Which Nobel Prize did Teresa of Calcutta receive in 1979?

a) peace   c) medicine

b) literature   d) economics

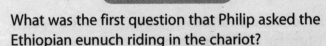

LEVEL 6

What was the first question that Philip asked the Ethiopian eunuch riding in the chariot?

a) "Do you understand what you are reading?"

b) "Do you speak Greek?"

c) "What do you have to do with the LORD, the God of Israel?"

d) "Do you think you will escape God's judgment?"

LEVEL 7

What city does Christian leave in John Bunyan's *The Pilgrim's Progress*?

a) city of the dead

b) Babylon

c) city of destruction

d) city of ignorance

Pages 197–199   Pages 213–218   Pages 233–235   Pages 245–247

SILVER

What special job did the district ruler in China give to Gladys Aylward?

- a) foot inspector
- b) tea taster
- c) mule skinner
- d) bookkeeper

LEVEL 9

Who was the Native American who became a Christian and gave assistance to the Plymouth Colony settlers?

- a) Squanto
- b) Aunt Queen
- c) Thomas Dusta
- d) Pocahontas

LEVEL 10

What phrase completes this statement by Hudson Taylor: "Under no circumstance would the missionary effort…"?

- a) "incur debt."
- b) "be done by unmarried female missionaries."
- c) "be conducted by married male missionaries."
- d) "accept funds from abroad."

Pages 200–202   Pages 219–224   Pages 236–238   Pages 248–250

LEVEL 11

What did Martha, the sister of Lazarus, do when she heard that Jesus was coming to their house?

    a) She dressed in a veil to receive Him.
    b) She cleaned the house.
    c) She went outside to meet Him.
    d) She started to cry.

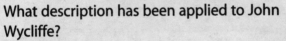

GOLD

What description has been applied to John Wycliffe?

    a) Lollard of Coventry
    b) Lion of Oxford
    c) morning star of the Reformation
    d) Luther's bulldog

Pages 203–204   Pages 225–228   Pages 239–240   Pages 251–252

QUIZ 9

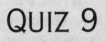

What phrase describes how "Jesus is calling" in
Will L. Thompson's song?

- a) "softly and tenderly"
- b) "with love divine"
- c) "with steadfast spirit"
- d) "with enduring mercy"

Page 193

Page 205

Page 229

Page 241

LEVEL 2

In what city did John Calvin develop his religious ideas?

    a) Venice, Italy
    b) Tübingen, Germany
    c) Paris, France
    d) Geneva, Switzerland

LEVEL 3

What was the question Nicodemus asked of Jesus?

    a) "Am I my brother's keeper?"
    b) "Sir, what must I do to be saved?"
    c) "How can a man be born when he is old?"
    d) "Tell me, are you a Roman citizen?"

BRONZE

In what area was Charles G. Finney's greatest success?

    a) providing assistance to the poor and
       suffering
    b) bringing the gospel to Native Americans
    c) as a revival evangelist
    d) organizing and promoting Sunday schools

Pages 194–196 Pages 207–212 Pages 230–232 Pages 242–244

LEVEL 5

Which Pharisee came to Jesus late at night?
- a) Joseph of Arimathea
- b) Zacchaeus
- c) Nicodemus
- d) James Zebedee

LEVEL 6

Who was the Christian scientist who stated the relationship between the pressure and volume of a gas?

- a) Marie Curie
- b) Humphry Davy
- c) William Perkin
- d) Robert Boyle

LEVEL 7

What kind of house is mentioned in the song "Let the Lower Lights Be Burning," by Philip P. Bliss?
- a) lighthouse
- b) farmhouse
- c) house of God
- d) house built on sand

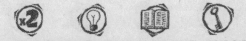

Pages 197–199   Pages 213–218   Pages 233–235   Pages 245–247

SILVER

How is Charles Sheldon's book *In His Steps* best described?

    a) a collection of sermons
    b) inspirational fiction
    c) a biography of Carry Nation
    d) one week in the life of a Christian
        newspaper editor

LEVEL 9

In her hymn "I Am Thine, O Lord," what appeal did Fanny J. Crosby make?

    a) "make me worthy"   c) "give me a mansion"
    b) "draw me nearer"   d) "keep me content"

LEVEL 10

What was the original title of the song "Amazing Grace" by John Newton?

    a) "Blinded in Youth by Satan's Arts"
    b) "Faith's Review and Expectation"
    c) "Be Still, My Heart! These Anxious Cares"
    d) "Alas! By Nature How Depraved"

Pages 200–202 Pages 219–224 Pages 236–238 Pages 248–250

LEVEL 11

Although she was British, Florence Nightingale was born in which country?
- a) Portugal
- b) Turkey
- c) Egypt
- d) Italy

GOLD

Astronaut James B. Irwin began what Christian evangelistic organization?
- a) Open Skies
- b) Chariots of Fire
- c) High Flight Foundation
- d) Scripture Memory Fellowship

Pages 203–204   Pages 225–228   Pages 239–240   Pages 251–252

THIRTY INTERACTIVE QUIZZES THAT PUT YOU IN THE HOT SEAT

TRIVIA
FOR
LIFE

QUIZ 10

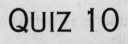

In Eugene M. Bartlett's song, what was found "in Jesus"?

  a) "the gates to life"
  b) "victory"
  c) "a lifeline"
  d) "sleep"

Page 193   Page 205   Page 229   Page 241

The book *In His Steps* by Charles Sheldon is the basis for what question?

    a) Will You bless me, too, my father?

    b) Am I my brother's keeper?

    c) What would Jesus do?

    d) Which is the greatest commandment in the Law?

What did the woman do who had been bleeding for twelve years?

    a) prepared Jesus a meal of bread, curds, and milk

    b) touched the edge of Jesus' cloak

    c) poured perfume on the head of Jesus

    d) washed the feet of Jesus with her hair

Pages 194–195   Pages 207–210   Pages 230–231   Pages 242–243

BRONZE

In his song, where does Russell Kelso Carter shout and sing that he is standing?

    a) in Canaan's land
    b) on the promises of God
    c) on streets of gold
    d) on Jordan's banks

LEVEL 5

Florence Nightingale's nursing activity is associated primarily with what war?

    a) Crimean War   c) Napoleonic Wars
    b) American Civil War   d) Boer War

LEVEL 6

What was the purpose of the underground to which Corrie ten Boom and her family belonged?

    a) to free slaves
    b) to provide a safe haven for Jews
    c) to transport German sympathizers
    d) to give gypsies a way to earn a living

Pages 196–198   Pages 211–216   Pages 232–234   Pages 244–246

LEVEL 7

The song "Jesus, Hold My Hand," by Albert E. Brumley, begins with what phrase?

   a) "As I travel through this pilgrim land"
   b) "Now I am climbing higher each day"
   c) "To a land where joy never ends"
   d) "I'm bound for that city"

SILVER

Where is Leonardo da Vinci's painting *The Last Supper* located?

   a) Royal Library, Windsor Castle, England
   b) Musée du Louvre, Paris
   c) Santa Maria delle Grazie in Milan, Italy
   d) the Sistine Chapel, Vatican, Italy

LEVEL 9

What word is missing from the phrase "___ of love" in Fanny J. Crosby's song "Blessed Assurance"?

   a) "song"   c) "light"
   b) "shadow"   d) "purchase"

Pages 199–201   Pages 217–222   Pages 235–237   Pages 247–249

LEVEL 10

Clara Barton's training and experience were in what field?

a) bookkeeping   c) nursing
b) school teaching   d) singing

LEVEL 11

What commendation did Enoch receive before he was taken from this life?

a) as one who pleased God
b) as a great warrior
c) as being a just king
d) as caring for his poor neighbors

GOLD

What African-American wrote "Peace in the Valley"?

a) Charles Richard Drew
b) Thomas A. Dorsey
c) Harriet Tubman
d) William C. Handy

Pages 202–204   Pages 223–228   Pages 238–240   Pages 250–252

THIRTY INTERACTIVE QUIZZES THAT PUT YOU IN THE HOT SEAT

TRIVIA
FOR
LIFE

QUIZ 11

What is the missing word from martyr Betty Scott Stam's motto: For to me, to live is Christ, and to die is _____?

a) victory
b) glory
c) power
d) gain

Page 193   Page 205   Page 229   Page 241

LEVEL 2

In Ira F. Stanphill's song "I Know Who Holds Tomorrow," what word completes the line "And I know who holds my..."?

a) "heart."   c) "future."
b) "hand."   d) "happiness."

LEVEL 3

Who was the Christian believer who stated the law of universal gravitation?

a) Isaac Newton
b) Galileo
c) Edmund Halley
d) John Hooke

BRONZE

From what is William W. Walford called in his song "Sweet Hour of Prayer"?

a) "from a life unaware"
b) "from a world of care"
c) "from an easy chair"
d) "from the Devil's snare"

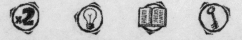

Pages 194–196   Pages 207–212   Pages 230–232   Pages 242–244

LEVEL 5

What was John Bunyan's position when he began writing *The Pilgrim's Progress*?

- a) vice chancellor at Oxford University
- b) prisoner in the Bedford, England, jail
- c) secretary of the admiralty in London
- d) soldier in Cromwell's army

LEVEL 6

From what region was the leper who came back to thank Jesus for his healing?

- a) Rome
- b) Samaria
- c) Galilee
- d) Egypt

LEVEL 7

What name could be applied to Brother Andrew (Andy van der Bijl)?

- a) Opponent of the Nazi Regime
- b) Great Revivalist
- c) Missionary to Liberia
- d) God's Undercover Agent

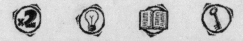

Pages 197–199   Pages 213–218   Pages 233–235   Pages 245–247

SILVER

For what purpose did Agabus take Paul's belt?
- a) to return it to Carpus at Troas who had loaned it to Paul
- b) to prophesy how Paul would be bound in Jerusalem
- c) to prevent Paul from leaving Caesarea
- d) to take it to Philip's four daughters so they could prophesy by touching it

LEVEL 9

What did Philip say to overcome his brother Nathaniel's disbelief that Jesus was the Messiah?
- a) "Never spake one like this."
- b) "Come and see."
- c) "He is like one crying in the wilderness."
- d) "He took away the sins of the world."

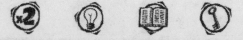

Pages 200–201   Pages 219–222   Pages 236–237   Pages 248–249

LEVEL 10

What did Ezra devote himself to?
- a) study and teaching the commands of God
- b) assembling a mighty army
- c) building a watchtower to protect the city
- d) tracing his lineage back to Adam

LEVEL 11

What was the name of Dante's fictionalized woman in *The Divine Comedy*?
- a) Deborah
- b) Gemma di Manetto Donati
- c) Veronica
- d) Beatrice

GOLD

Who was the Christian believer who showed that light is made of electromagnetic waves?
- a) James Clerk Maxwell
- b) Christian Huygens
- c) Albert Michelson
- d) John Dalton

Pages 202–204   Pages 223–228   Pages 238–240   Pages 250–252

THIRTY INTERACTIVE QUIZZES THAT PUT YOU IN THE HOT SEAT

TRIVIA FOR LIFE

QUIZ 12

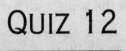

For what activity is evangelist Charles Wesley known?

- a) organizing congregations
- b) writing hymns
- c) translating the works of Martin Luther
- d) delivering sermons

Page 193   Page 205   Page 229   Page 241

LEVEL 2

The hymn "When the Roll Is Called Up Yonder" by James Milton Black mentions what musical instrument in the first line?

   a) cymbals   c) trumpet

   b) lyre   d) harp

LEVEL 3

In the James Rowe song "Love Lifted Me," what was he far from?

   a) "the peaceful shore"   c) "cliff of the rock"

   b) "home of the soul"   d) "lights of home"

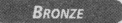

BRONZE

What did God state about Eve's offspring?

   a) That He would crush the serpent's head.

   b) That He would be a little lower than the angels.

   c) That He would begin a people too numerous to count.

   d) That He would be called a "son of the living God."

Pages 194–196   Pages 207–212   Pages 230–232   Pages 242–244

LEVEL 5

In what country did William Carey serve for forty-one years?

a) India   c) Africa
b) China   d) Canada

LEVEL 6

Who was the Christian believer and great scientist who discovered a vaccination for rabies?

a) Joseph Lister   c) Roger Bacon
b) Edward Jenner   d) Louis Pasteur

LEVEL 7

What response did the woman of Canaan give when Jesus said He was sent to the lost sheep of Israel?

a) "The shepherd leaves the ninety-nine and goes after the lost sheep."
b) "I give half of my possessions to the poor."
c) "It is not the healthy who need a doctor, but the sick."
d) "Even the dogs eat the crumbs that fall from their masters' table."

Pages 197–199   Pages 213–218   Pages 233–235   Pages 245–247

SILVER

Because they were both from Scotland and worked in textile mills as children, who did Mary Slessor identify with as her exemplar missionary?

a) Hudson Taylor   c) David Livingstone
b) Gladys Aylward   d) George Müller

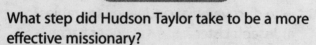

LEVEL 9

What step did Hudson Taylor take to be a more effective missionary?

a) He dressed as a native teacher.
b) He built a walled city as a Christian stronghold.
c) He translated Chinese literature into English.
d) He used puppet plays to tell the story of Jesus.

LEVEL 10

What condition did English poet William Cowper, author of "There Is a Fountain," struggle with?

a) alcoholism   c) depression
b) blindness   d) deafness

Pages 200–202   Pages 219–224   Pages 236–238   Pages 248–250

LEVEL 11

William Carey had exceptional ability in what position?
- a) school superintendent
- b) translator
- c) governor
- d) hospital administrator

GOLD

How did Dietrich Bonhoeffer die?
- a) of pneumonia while an honored guest in Britain
- b) by hanging at a concentration camp
- c) at home during the bombing of Berlin
- d) aboard a ship sunk by a U-boat

Pages 203–204   Pages 225–228   Pages 239–240   Pages 251–252

THIRTY INTERACTIVE QUIZZES THAT PUT YOU IN THE HOT SEAT •

TRIVIA FOR LIFE

QUIZ 13

LEVEL 1

Who is the title character in *The Screwtape Letters* by C. S. Lewis?

    a) an experienced devil
    b) the nephew of the letter writer
    c) an English linguist named Ransom
    d) C. S. Lewis himself

Page 193

Page 205

Page 229

Page 241

LEVEL 2

What did John the Baptist eat in the wilderness?
- a) fish
- b) bread and water
- c) locusts and wild honey
- d) figs and pomegranates

LEVEL 3

What organization did William and Catherine Booth found?
- a) Teen Challenge
- b) Red Cross
- c) YMCA
- d) Salvation Army

BRONZE

In the song "Farther Along" by W. B. Stevens, what follows "Cheer up my brother"?
- a) "every step is getting brighter"
- b) "look to realms above"
- c) "live in the sunshine"
- d) "soon we'll reach the shining river"

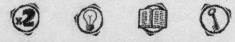

Pages 194–196   Pages 207–212   Pages 230–232   Pages 242–244

LEVEL 5

Gladys Aylward served in what occupation before going to China?

    a) a nurse   c) a maid
    b) a schoolteacher d) an actress

LEVEL 6

Why did Rhoda delay opening the door when Peter escaped from prison?

    a) She feared the Romans.
    b) She thought he was a ghost.
    c) She thought she would be laughed at.
    d) She was overjoyed.

LEVEL 7

What was the first public message sent by Samuel F. B. Morse's telegraph?

    a) "What hath God wrought!"
    b) the words of "Silent Night"
    c) "Lord, who has believed our message?"
    d) "Your lightning lit up the world."

Pages 197–199   Pages 213–218   Pages 233–235   Pages 245–247

SILVER

How old was Anna when she saw Jesus in the temple?

   a) 12 years old   c) 40 years old
   b) 33 years old   d) 84 years old

LEVEL 9

Dietrich Bonhoeffer was an outspoken leader of which church that opposed Hitler and Nazism?

   a) Non-Aryan Christian Church
   b) German Evangelical Church
   c) National Socialist Church
   d) Confessing Church

LEVEL 10

Why was Hezekiah like no king of Judah either before or after him?

   a) Only God was held in greater respect by the people.
   b) He followed the Lord and kept the commands given to Moses.
   c) He did evil in the eyes of the Lord continually.
   d) Peace reigned throughout Canaan.

Pages 200–202   Pages 219–224   Pages 236–238   Pages 248–250

LEVEL 11

Which of these heroes of faith did not experience death?

  a) Samson
  b) Enoch
  c) Gideon
  d) Jacob

GOLD

Edith Schaeffer's first book about her and her husband's work in Switzerland carried what title?

  a) *Children for Christ*
  b) *Defending the Faith*
  c) *The Tapestry*
  d) *L'Abri* (the shelter)

Pages 203–204   Pages 225–228   Pages 239–240   Pages 251–252

THIRTY INTERACTIVE QUIZZES THAT PUT YOU IN THE HOT SEAT

TRIVIA
FOR
LIFE

QUIZ 14

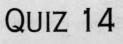

Why did Joseph continue with his plans to take Mary as his wife?

    a) he had a visit from an angel
    b) to escape the wrath of the village elders
    c) to inherit her extensive dowry
    d) to fulfill a promise he had given her father

Page 193

Page 205

Page 229

Page 241

Who named all the animals on earth?
   a) Shem's sons at Babel
   b) Adam
   c) God
   d) Noah

What is the title of Jonathan Edwards's sermon that says "there is nothing between you and Hell but the air"?
   a) "True Virtue"
   b) "A Strict Enquiry into Notions of Freedom of Will"
   c) "Sinners in the Hands of an Angry God"
   d) "God Glorified in Man's Dependence"

BRONZE

What was Andrew's relation to Simon Peter?
   a) hired servant   c) son
   b) father   d) brother

Pages 194–196   Pages 207–212   Pages 230–232   Pages 242–244

LEVEL 5

In what war did Clara Barton earn the title "angel of the battlefield"?

    a) Spanish-American War
    b) American Civil War
    c) World War I
    d) Franco-Prussian War

LEVEL 6

After learning that Jesus was the Messiah, what did Andrew do?

    a) asked to be healed
    b) told his brother
    c) asked to sit on Jesus' right hand
    d) fished all night

LEVEL 7

Francis Schaeffer is noted for defending the historical accuracy of what portion of Scripture?

    a) The biblical account of Moses
    b) Genesis 1–11
    c) The biblical account of Jesus
    d) The biblical account of Abraham

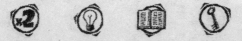

Pages 197–199   Pages 213–218   Pages 233–235   Pages 245–247

SILVER

Who watched baby Moses while he was being hidden from Pharaoh?

- a) his father
- b) his brother Aaron
- c) his sister Miriam
- d) his grandmother

LEVEL 9

How is Samuel Morris (Prince Kaboo) described on his memorial at Taylor University?

- a) Liberator of Liberia
- b) King of Missionaries
- c) Man Without a Country
- d) Apostle of Simple Faith

LEVEL 10

Of what religious movement was George Whitefield one of the leaders?

- a) Protestant Reformation
- b) Great Awakening
- c) Moderate Sensibility
- d) Backwoods Revivalism

Pages 200–202   Pages 219–224   Pages 236–238   Pages 248–250

LEVEL 11

What title could be used to describe Luis Palau's early ministry?

    a) The Singing Cowboy
    b) Argentina's hymn writer
    c) Evangelist of Latin America
    d) Survivor of the Inquisition

GOLD

What was the primary reason Frederick Douglass wrote *Narrative of the Life of Frederick Douglass*?

    a) to establish himself as a writer
    b) to help locate his family
    c) to provide specific details of his life to
       prove that he had been a slave
    d) to raise money for abolitionist causes

Pages 203–204   Pages 225–228   Pages 239–240   Pages 251–252

THIRTY INTERACTIVE QUIZZES THAT PUT YOU IN THE HOT SEAT

TRIVIA
FOR
LIFE

QUIZ 15

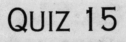

Brother Andrew (Andy van der Bijl) first smuggled Bibles into what part of the world?
    a) behind the Iron Curtain
    b) Red China
    c) the Muslim world
    d) Africa

Page 193

Page 206

Page 229

Page 241

What words of Jesus does Leonardo da Vinci illustrate with *The Last Supper*?

    a) "The Christ will suffer and rise from the dead on the third day."

    b) "Unless I wash you, you have no part with me."

    c) "Before the rooster crows, you will disown me three times."

    d) "One of you will betray me—one who is eating with me."

In Charles Wesley's song "Hark, the Herald Angels Sing," what do the angels sing?

    a) "a new song in heaven"

    b) "everyone is waiting the coming day"

    c) "take time to praise the Lord"

    d) "glory to the newborn King"

Pages 194–195   Pages 207–210   Pages 230–231   Pages 242–243

BRONZE

What physical condition affected Fanny J. Crosby?
    a) severe depression
    b) quadriplegia
    c) muscular dystrophy
    d) blindness

LEVEL 5

Who was the three-time presidential candidate who wrote "The Bible and Its Enemies"?
    a) Jimmy Carter
    b) James Garfield
    c) James Buchanan
    d) William Jennings Bryan

LEVEL 6

What was the source of George Müller's salary?
    a) unsolicited freewill offerings
    b) his father's dynamite business
    c) his many best-selling books
    d) his wife's inheritance

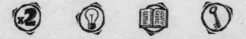

Pages 196–198   Pages 211–216   Pages 232–234   Pages 244–246

LEVEL 7

Who was Zipporah's husband, whom she
described as "an Egyptian" when they first met?

a) Moses   c) Noah
b) Joshua   d) Joseph

SILVER

In the William Cowper song that has the phrase
"His wonders to perform," how does he say that
God moves?

a) "with an easy yoke"
b) "softly and tenderly"
c) "in a mysterious way"
d) "as footprints in the sand"

LEVEL 9

What organization did George Müller found?

a) The Navigators
b) Scriptural Knowledge Institution
c) National Home Education Association
d) Society of Friends

Pages 199–201   Pages 217–222   Pages 235–237   Pages 247–249

LEVEL 10

The well where Jesus talked with a woman of Samaria was named after what Old Testament person?

    a) Noah   c) Gideon
    b) Jonah   d) Jacob

LEVEL 11

George Washington Carver said, "_____ is an unlimited broadcasting system through which God speaks to us every hour, if we will only tune in."

    a) "Nature"   c) "The Bible"
    b) "Prayer"   d) "The starry sky"

GOLD

By what name were Charles Wesley and his friends known at Oxford University?

    a) Wesley's Party   c) Faithful Brethren
    b) Holy Club   d) Singing Saints

Pages 202–204   Pages 223–228   Pages 238–240   Pages 250–252

THIRTY INTERACTIVE QUIZZES THAT PUT YOU IN THE HOT SEAT

TRIVIA
FOR
LIFE

QUIZ 16

LEVEL 1

What term did Teresa of Calcutta use for the poor, sick, and suffering?

a) street people
b) slum brothers and sisters
c) Christ in disguise
d) congregation of the destitute

Page 193

Page 206

Page 229

Page 241

LEVEL 2

What is the subtitle of the book *Ben Hur* by Lew Wallace?

    a) *A Tale of the Christ*
    b) *The First Christmas*
    c) *The Chariot Race*
    d) *A Prince of Israel*

LEVEL 3

What did God tell Abraham about Sarah?

    a) Her son would be a joy and delight.
    b) The Spirit of God would come upon her.
    c) She would be the mother of nations.
    d) She had found favor with God.

BRONZE

What was Abel's occupation?

    a) laborer in the fields
    b) mighty warrior
    c) tender of vineyards
    d) keeper of flocks

Pages 194–196   Pages 207–212   Pages 230–232   Pages 242–244

LEVEL 5

While in a trance, what did Peter hear God tell him to do?
- a) stay awake until the rooster crowed
- b) fast for forty days
- c) warm himself by the enemy's fire
- d) kill and eat unclean animals

LEVEL 6

How did William Tyndale die?
- a) he was strangled and burned at the stake
- b) of an illness while visiting the Holy Land
- c) ill treatment while in prison
- d) lost at sea while transporting New Testaments to England

LEVEL 7

In Robert Lowry's song "Beautiful River" ("Shall We Gather at the River"), whose feet trod along the river?
- a) bright angel
- c) wayfaring pilgrims
- b) Son of God
- d) those marching to Zion

Pages 197–199   Pages 213–218   Pages 233–235   Pages 245–247

What did Edward "Buzz" Aldrin do when he and Neil Armstrong landed on the moon on Sunday, July 20, 1969?

    a) read the "In the beginning" passage from Genesis

    b) observed the Lord's Supper

    c) recited the Lord's Prayer

    d) sang a hymn

Why did Hannah choose the name Samuel for her son?

    a) It means "hairy"—his appearance.

    b) It means "perfection of the father"—he favored his father.

    c) It means "brother of Ramuel"—his twin sister.

    d) It means "asked of the LORD"—she prayed for a son.

Pages 200–201 Pages 219–222 Pages 236–237 Pages 248–249

LEVEL 10

According to the writer of Hebrews, Abraham looked for what kind of city?

a) "a city on a hill"
b) "the city of the living God"
c) "a holy city with the tree of life"
d) "a city whose architect and builder is God"

LEVEL 11

A. W. Tozer is the author of what book?

a) *Institutes of the Christian Religion*
b) *How to Be Born Again*
c) *The Pursuit of God*
d) *A Fully Surrendered Man*

GOLD

What happened when Sojourner Truth brought suit in court for the return of her son, who had been sold into slavery in Alabama?

a) She lost and had to pay court cost.
b) She won the case.
c) Her case was dismissed without merit.
d) It went for years without resolution.

Pages 202–204   Pages 223–228   Pages 238–240   Pages 250–252

THIRTY INTERACTIVE QUIZZES THAT PUT YOU IN THE HOT SEAT

TRIVIA
FOR
LIFE

QUIZ 17

What Scripture prompted Martin Luther to say,
"At this I felt myself to have been born again"?

   a) "This water symbolizes baptism that now
      saves you also."

   b) "And those He predestined, He also called."

   c) "If God is for us, who can be against us?"

   d) "The righteous will live by faith."

Page 193   Page 206   Page 229   Page 241

LEVEL 2

What is Florence Nightingale often portrayed carrying?

    a) pitcher of water   c) lamp

    b) medical kit   d) Bible

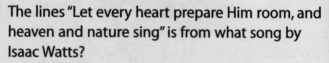

LEVEL 3

The lines "Let every heart prepare Him room, and heaven and nature sing" is from what song by Isaac Watts?

    a) "I'm Not Ashamed to Own My Lord"

    b) "How Shall the Young Secure Their Hearts"

    c) "There Is a Land of Pure Delight"

    d) "Joy to the World"

BRONZE

In the Martin Luther hymn "A Mighty Fortress Is Our God," how does he identify the devil?

    a) "our ancient foe"

    b) "Lucifer"

    c) "sly fox"

    d) "Legion"

Pages 194–196 Pages 207–212 Pages 230–232 Pages 242–244

LEVEL 5

What best-selling book did Dale Evans write about Robin, her daughter with Down's Syndrome?

- a) *Pals of the Golden West*
- b) *Angel Unaware*
- c) *Just Sing a Song*
- d) *The Day That We Met Jesus*

LEVEL 6

To what does Albert E. Brumley liken himself in his song "He Set Me Free"?

- a) bird in prison
- b) a worm
- c) a lost sheep
- d) a lily of the valley

LEVEL 7

What six-thousand-seat auditorium was built for Charles Haddon Spurgeon?

- a) Royal Albert Hall
- b) Metropolitan Tabernacle
- c) the Globe Theater
- d) the Crystal Palace

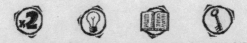

Pages 197–199   Pages 213–218   Pages 233–235   Pages 245–247

What do Susanna, Joanna, and Mary Magdalene have in common?
- a) They all belonged to the household of Herod.
- b) They were lepers.
- c) They helped support Jesus and the disciples.
- d) They encouraged their husbands in the faith.

What did Gideon call the altar he built?
- a) "Here Is Faith"
- b) "The LORD Is Peace"
- c) "The Place I Saw an Angel"
- d) "The Wisdom of God"

LEVEL 10

Who said, "He told me everything I ever did"?
- a) nobleman whose son was sick at Capernaum
- b) demon-possessed man from the tombs
- c) Samaritan woman who met Jesus at the well
- d) centurion whose servant was sick

Pages 200–202 Pages 219–224 Pages 236–238 Pages 248–250

Why did Frederick Douglass go to England in 1859?
- a) to escape the danger of seizure under the Fugitive Slave Laws
- b) to gain support for the American Civil War
- c) to avoid possible arrest because of John Brown's raid at Harpers Ferry
- d) to raise money for Abraham Lincoln's campaign for president

Why did Andy van der Bijl minister under the name Brother Andrew?
- a) to be harder to trace as he moved about an unfriendly country
- b) to appear to be a local resident
- c) because he admired Andrew in the Bible
- d) to put his past behind him and start fresh

Pages 203–204   Pages 225–228   Pages 239–240   Pages 251–252

THIRTY INTERACTIVE QUIZZES THAT PUT YOU IN THE HOT SEAT

TRIVIA
FOR
LIFE

QUIZ 18

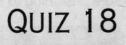
LEVEL 1

What movie chronicles the story of Eric Liddell's
Olympic triumphs?
   a) *Wings*
   b) *A Step Farther*
   c) *Chariots of Fire*
   d) *Triumph of Will*

Page 193   Page 206   Page 229   Page 241

LEVEL 2

What was the name of the mother of John the Baptist?

    a) Anna   c) Elizabeth

    b) Joanna   d) Tabitha

LEVEL 3

Who said "I will fear no evil"?

    a) Noah as the rains descended

    b) David in one of his psalms

    c) John the Baptist when thrown into prison

    d) Jonah before preaching to Nineveh

BRONZE

In the Roy Rogers and Dale Evans song, what follows the opening words of "Happy trails to you..."

    a) "for a life that is true."

    b) "until we meet again."

    c) "it's the way you ride the trail that counts."

    d) "who cares about the clouds."

Pages 194–196   Pages 207–212   Pages 230–232   Pages 242–244

LEVEL 5

Whom did the Lord describe to Satan as "There is no one on earth like him; he is blameless and upright"?

a) David   c) Job
b) Moses   d) Noah

LEVEL 6

What person, known as the Father of Modern Missions, was trained as a shoemaker?

a) C. S. Lewis   c) David Livingstone
b) Billy Graham   d) William Carey

LEVEL 7

In the William J. and Gloria Gaither song "Jesus Is Lord of All," what two times are mentioned in the first line?

a) "the years and the ages"
b) "all my tomorrows, all my past"
c) "ages roll through eternity's scroll"
d) "a time to be born and a time to die"

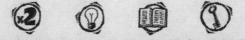

Pages 197–199   Pages 213–218   Pages 233–235   Pages 245–247

SILVER

In addition to being an explorer and missionary, what was another of David Livingstone's occupations?

    a) veterinarian

    b) newspaper reporter

    c) physician

    d) songwriter

LEVEL 9

After being dismissed from his congregation in Northampton, Massachusetts, Jonathan Edwards served in what capacity?

    a) as a newspaper editor in Philadelphia

    b) as a naturalist growing new varieties
       of potatoes

    c) as a missionary to Native Americans

    d) as a translator of Luther's works from
       the German language

Pages 200–201   Pages 219–222   Pages 236–237   Pages 248–249

LEVEL 10

Who wrote the book *Institutes of the Christian Religion,* which helped establish Protestantism?
   a) Martin Luther   c) Ulrich Zwingli
   b) John Calvin   d) John Knox

LEVEL 11

What did Abraham do when God said his wife, Sarah, would have a son?
   a) moved from Ur of the Chaldeans to Canaan
   b) sacrificed a ram
   c) built an altar to the LORD
   d) fell facedown and laughed

GOLD

Why did Paul refer to Phoebe as "our sister"?
   a) She managed a home for orphans.
   b) She was a servant of the church.
   c) She was charitable to everyone.
   d) She was Paul's half sister.

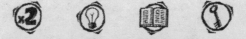

Pages 202–204   Pages 223–228   Pages 238–240   Pages 250–252

THIRTY INTERACTIVE QUIZZES THAT PUT YOU IN THE HOT SEAT

TRIVIA
FOR
LIFE

QUIZ 19

LEVEL 1

Where did Moses receive the Ten Commandments from God?
- a) Mount Carmel
- b) Mount Horeb
- c) mountains of Ararat
- d) Mount Sinai

Page 193

Page 206

Page 229

Page 241

LEVEL 2

What words are missing from this song by
Thomas A. Dorsey: "Precious Lord, __ __ __, lead
me on"?

    a) "thru the night"   c) "take my hand"

    b) "thru the storm"   d) "to the light"

LEVEL 3

In his song "Soldiers of Christ, Arise," what does
Charles Wesley tell soldiers of Christ to do?

    a) "march to Zion"

    b) "sing Hail to the Risen Lord"

    c) "to Christ be loyal"

    d) "put your armor on"

BRONZE

In Gloria Gaither's song "Something Beautiful,"
what did "He" understand?

    a) "how to help us find our way"

    b) "all my confusion"

    c) "kings and kingdoms"

    d) "battlefields of my own making"

Pages 194–196   Pages 207–212   Pages 230–232   Pages 242–244

Johannes Kepler was a Christian who made what scientific discovery?
- a) the three laws of planetary motion
- b) matter is made of atoms
- c) the principle of the pendulum
- d) the speed of light in a vacuum

What doctrine did John Wesley and his brother emphasize?
- a) contending for the faith
- b) predestination
- c) faith and the pursuit of holiness
- d) universal salvation

What book, the first he wrote, is the starting point for understanding Francis Schaeffer's theology?
- a) *A Christian View of Ecology*
- b) *The God Who Is There*
- c) *False Antithesis*
- d) *A Christian Manifesto*

Pages 197–199   Pages 213–218   Pages 233–235   Pages 245–247

SILVER

What did Samuel of the Old Testament answer when he realized the Lord was calling him?

    a) "Here I am; you called me."

    b) "What shall I do, Lord?"

    c) "O Lord, please send someone else."

    d) "Speak, for your servant is listening."

LEVEL 9

In addition to being a prophetess, what else is true about Deborah of the Old Testament?

    a) She was the wife of Solomon.

    b) She led Israel.

    c) She was a priestess.

    d) She earned a living by gleaning grain.

LEVEL 10

The line "and the white robed angels sing the story" is from what Charles Austin Miles song?

    a) "A New Name in Glory"

    b) "Look for Me!"

    c) "I'm Going There"

    d) "Dwelling in Beulah Land"

Pages 200–202   Pages 219–224   Pages 236–238   Pages 248–250

LEVEL 11

What was the purpose of Susanna Wesley's strong discipline and instruction for her children?

　　a) for a vocation worthy of a Wesley
　　b) for the saving of their souls
　　c) for acquiring a measure of riches
　　d) for their success as ministers

GOLD

What did Agabus prophesy when Paul was in Antioch?

　　a) a marriage in Cana
　　b) a great fire in Rome
　　c) Jesus' death
　　d) a severe famine

Pages 203–204　Pages 225–228　Pages 239–240　Pages 251–252

QUIZ 20

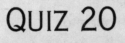
LEVEL 1

What is Billy Graham's primary focus in modern Christianity?
- a) evangelism
- b) foreign missions
- c) song writing
- d) philanthropy

Page 193   Page 206   Page 229   Page 241

LEVEL 2

What name was later given to the type of worship John Wesley and his brother began while at the University of Oxford?

a) Puritanism   c) Moravianism
b) Wesleyism   d) Methodism

LEVEL 3

What career did Billy Sunday have before becoming a minister?

a) professional baseball player
b) schoolteacher
c) telegraph operator
d) lumberjack

BRONZE

How is the book *The Pilgrim's Progress* by John Bunyan best described?

a) memoirs of a missionary
b) historical novel
c) devotional book
d) allegory

Pages 194–196   Pages 207–212   Pages 230–232   Pages 242–244

LEVEL 5

Sir Christopher Wren is noted for what accomplishment?
- a) discovery of the planet Neptune
- b) astronomer of the southern skies
- c) author of *The Faerie Queene*
- d) architect of Saint Paul's cathedral, London

LEVEL 6

Michael Faraday was a Christian who invented what important device?
- a) telephone
- b) solid fuel rocket
- c) electric motor
- d) precision chronometer

LEVEL 7

Who wrote *Paradise Regained,* the sequel to John Milton's *Paradise Lost*?
- a) Francis Bacon
- b) John Milton
- c) Samuel Pepys
- d) John Bunyan

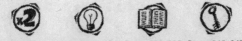

Pages 197–199   Pages 213–218   Pages 233–235   Pages 245–247

SILVER

What is the name of the ministry that Brother Andrew (Andy van der Bijl) founded?

    a) Bibles Without Borders

    b) Open Doors

    c) Undercover Missionaries

    d) The Red Letter Edition

LEVEL 9

Why did Jezebel and Ahab have Naboth stoned to death?

    a) because the Lord had commanded it

    b) for his vineyard

    c) to please those they ruled

    d) because he preached against their marriage

LEVEL 10

Charles Wesley uses the phrase "Sons of men and angels say" in which song?

    a) "Christ the Lord Is Risen Today"

    b) "Jesus Loves the Castaway"

    c) "Rejoice, the Devil Is in Disarray"

    d) "Love Divine, All Love Without Delay"

Pages 200–202　　Pages 219–224　　Pages 236–238　　Pages 248–250

LEVEL 11

In the song "Whispering Hope" by Alice Hawthorne (pseudonym of Septimus Winner), how is the voice of the angel described?

a) "hushed"
b) "soft"
c) "rejoicing"
d) "sweet"

GOLD

Although he rejected labels, under what name did Watchman Nee's ministry become known?

a) Cottage Christian Movement
b) Little Flock Movement
c) Three Self Movement
d) Great Leap Forward

Pages 203–204   Pages 225–228   Pages 239–240   Pages 251–252

THIRTY INTERACTIVE QUIZZES THAT PUT YOU IN THE HOT SEAT

TRIVIA
FOR
LIFE

QUIZ 21

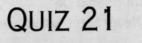

In William Cowper's song "There Is a Fountain,"
what fills the fountain?

a) "blood"
b) "balm"
c) "a healing stream"
d) "peace"

Page 193

Page 206

Page 229

Page 241

LEVEL 2

Whom was Paul talking about when he said, "Our dear friend, the doctor"?

a) Levi   c) Luke

b) Lydia   d) Lot

LEVEL 3

The greeting of "How do you do" is in which Albert E. Brumley song?

a) "Down in Memory Valley"

b) "I'll Meet You in the Morning"

c) "Turn Your Radio On"

d) "If We Never Meet Again"

BRONZE

In Leonardo da Vinci's *Last Supper,* what is Judas Iscariot holding?

a) a bag of money

b) an upside down cross

c) a dagger

d) a piece of bread

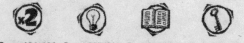

Pages 194–196 Pages 207–212 Pages 230–232 Pages 242–244

LEVEL 5

The unfinished fragments of Blaise Pascal's proposed book *Apology [Defense] of the Christian Religion* were published as what book?

   a) *De la fréquente communion*
       (Frequent Communion)
   b) *Pensées sur la religion*
       (Thoughts on Religion)
   c) *L'honnêteté* (Polite Respectability)
   d) *Lettres provinciales* (Provincial Letters)

LEVEL 6

What is the title of the Frances Havergal song with the words "consecrated, Lord, to Thee"?

   a) "Is It for Me?"
   b) "Another Year Is Dawning"
   c) "Take My Life, and Let It Be"
   d) "I Bring My Sins to Thee"

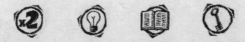

Pages 197–198   Pages 213–216   Pages 233–234   Pages 245–246

LEVEL 7

What word completes this statement by missionary martyr Jim Elliot: "He is no fool who gives what he cannot keep to gain what he cannot..."?

   a) "see."   c) "find."

   b) "lose."   d) "understand."

SILVER

Who wrote *Out of the Silent Planet,* a book that fused science fiction and religious allegory?

   a) G. K. Chesterton   c) John Milton

   b) J. R. R. Tolkien   d) C. S. Lewis

LEVEL 9

Hudson Taylor interrupted his work on what advanced degree to go to China?

   a) Doctor of Fine Arts

   b) Doctor of Medicine

   c) Doctor of Divinity

   d) Doctor of Music

Pages 199–201   Pages 217–222   Pages 235–237   Pages 247–249

LEVEL 10

What is the title of Mahalia Jackson's autobiography?

    a) *Movin' On*
    b) *Queen of Gospel Song*
    c) *We Shall Overcome*
    d) *Hope Is the Hallmark*

LEVEL 11

Besides keeping sheep, what did Amos of the Old Testament take care of before the Lord called him to prophesy?

    a) a rich merchant's business
    b) the king's stables
    c) the tabernacle
    d) sycamore-fig trees

GOLD

Who was the founder of modern surgery who said, "I treated him; God healed him"?

    a) Joseph Lister   c) Louis Pasteur
    b) William T. G. Morton   d) Ambroise Paré

Pages 202–204 Pages 223–228 Pages 238–240 Pages 250–252

THIRTY INTERACTIVE QUIZZES THAT PUT YOU IN THE HOT SEAT

TRIVIA FOR LIFE

QUIZ 22

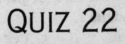

Martin Luther is considered the father of what upheaval?

a) Protestant Reformation
b) Great Awakening
c) Great Schism
d) German Renaissance

Page 193   Page 206   Page 229   Page 241

LEVEL 2

What was the religious ministry of Dwight L. Moody?

a) upholding Genesis against secular humanism
b) serving as president of the Moody Bible Institute
c) evangelism
d) writing Bible commentaries

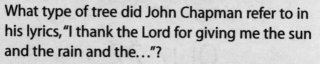

LEVEL 3

What type of tree did John Chapman refer to in his lyrics, "I thank the Lord for giving me the sun and the rain and the…"?

a) "apple tree."
b) "family tree."
c) "tree of knowledge."
d) "tree of life."

BRONZE

Which book by C. S. Lewis has Aslan, a Christlike character, in it?

a) *The Screwtape Letters*
b) *The Lion, the Witch and the Wardrobe*
c) *Surprised by Joy*
d) *Shadowlands*

Pages 194–196   Pages 207–212   Pages 230–232   Pages 242–244

LEVEL 5

How could Billy Sunday's religious beliefs be described?

a) ecumenical   c) fundamental
b) pentecostal   d) liberal

LEVEL 6

What did Jesus say as the widow gave two very small copper coins to the temple treasury?

a) "For with the measure you use, it will be measured to you."
b) "One coin would have been sufficient."
c) "It is hard for a rich person to enter the kingdom of heaven."
d) "This poor widow has put in more than all the others."

LEVEL 7

What color is associated with Lydia?

a) green   c) blue
b) purple   d) black

SILVER

What word completes the first line of Frances Havergal's song "True-hearted, whole-hearted, faithful and..."?

a) "glorious."   c) "regal."
b) "loyal."   d) "meek."

LEVEL 9

After Jacob kissed Rachel and began weeping aloud, what did she do?

a) said, "You are my own flesh and blood."
b) began to weep, too
c) gave him her family idols
d) ran and told her father, Laban

LEVEL 10

What was one of Charles G. Finney's "new measures" for which he received criticism?

a) strict interpretation of predestination
b) the call for a public response to receive Christ after he finished preaching
c) refusal to allow public outbursts of emotion
d) preaching without singing or prayer

Pages 200–202   Pages 219–224   Pages 236–238   Pages 248–249

LEVEL 11

How did Mahalia Jackson describe gospel music?
- a) as songs of the sanctified church
- b) as songs of fear and faith
- c) as songs of the people
- d) as songs of hope

GOLD

What was Dwight L. Moody's first success as a Christian?
- a) comforting soldiers during the Civil War
- b) showing businessmen in England how to serve Jesus
- c) preaching to prisoners at the Tombs in New York City
- d) starting Sunday schools for slum children in Chicago

Pages 203–204   Pages 225–228   Pages 239–240   Pages 251–252

THIRTY INTERACTIVE QUIZZES THAT PUT YOU IN THE HOT SEAT

TRIVIA
FOR
LIFE

QUIZ 23

LEVEL 1

The words "Troublesome times are here, filling men's hearts with fear" are from what Robert E. Winsett song?

    a) "The Message"
    b) "Living by Faith"
    c) "Jesus Is Coming Soon"
    d) "Hallelujah! We Shall Rise"

Page 193   Page 206   Page 229   Page 241

LEVEL 2

What instrument is mentioned in the song "The King Is Coming" by Gloria Gaither, William J. Gaither, and Charles Milhuff?

   a) cymbal   c) lyre
   b) harp   d) trumpet

LEVEL 3

Who is directly credited with writing thirty-seven of the Psalms and probably wrote many others?

   a) David
   b) Abraham
   c) Moses
   d) Solomon

BRONZE

What phrase is found in the song "Send the Light" by Charles H. Gabriel?

   a) "No clouds in heaven a shadow to cast"
   b) "I'm pressing on the upward way"
   c) "There are souls to rescue"
   d) "O that will be glory"

Pages 194–196   Pages 207–212   Pages 230–232   Pages 242–244

LEVEL 5

Which of the following worshipers of God could be described as a businesswoman?
- a) Drusilla
- b) Phoebe
- c) Ruth
- d) Lydia

LEVEL 6

Why did Pocahontas (Matoaka) change her name to Rebecca?
- a) English settlers found it easier to pronounce.
- b) She took the name after becoming a Christian.
- c) To pass for an European while in England.
- d) So her father could not find her when she adopted English ways.

LEVEL 7

Who was the one who carried the news of the risen Lord to the disciples?
- a) Rhoda
- b) Mary of Bethany
- c) Mary Magdalene
- d) Mary the mother of Jesus

Pages 197–199   Pages 213–218   Pages 233–235   Pages 245–247

How did the four who carried the paralyzed man bring him before Jesus?

   a) lowered him through an opening made in the roof

   b) waited on the road to Jericho

   c) lowered him in a basket from a sycamore-fig tree

   d) waited for Jesus by a well

LEVEL 9

Which songbook was written by Isaac Watts?

   a) *Olney Hymns*

   b) *Pocket Hymnbook for the Use of Christians of All Denominations*

   c) *First Book of Songs or Ayres*

   d) *Hymns and Spiritual Songs*

LEVEL 10

What musical instrument did Miriam, Aaron's sister, play?

   a) horn   c) flute

   b) harp   d) tambourine

Pages 200–202   Pages 219–224   Pages 236–238   Pages 248–250

LEVEL 11

The statement "For nothing is impossible with God" referred to what miracle?

   a) salvation for the Gentiles
   b) raising the dead
   c) the virgin birth of Jesus
   d) Elizabeth becoming a mother

GOLD

In her best-known speech, what question did Sojourner Truth ask?

   a) "Am I not a graduate from slavery with a diploma on my back?"
   b) "How is it that we hear the loudest yelps for liberty from the drivers of slaves?"
   c) "Ain't I a woman?"
   d) "Did you do anything to lessen my load?"

Pages 203–204   Pages 225–228   Pages 239–240   Pages 251–252

THIRTY INTERACTIVE QUIZZES THAT PUT YOU IN THE HOT SEAT

TRIVIA
FOR
LIFE

QUIZ 24

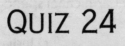

LEVEL 1

How was John Newton first employed?
 a) as a surveyor for the Liverpool shipyards
 b) as a minister in Olney, England
 c) as a gunpowder salesman
 d) as a sailor engaged in slave trading

Page 193   Page 206   Page 229   Page 241

LEVEL 2

What did Jesus say to Peter in calling him as a disciple?

- a) "The harvest is plentiful but the workers are few."
- b) "It is not the healthy who need a doctor, but the sick."
- c) "Go rather to the lost sheep of Israel."
- d) "I will make you fishers of men."

LEVEL 3

Where did Amy Carmichael spend fifty-six years as a missionary?

- a) China
- b) Africa
- c) India
- d) Indonesia

BRONZE

How did God react to Abel's offerings?

- a) He said, "Your burnt offerings are not acceptable."
- b) God spoke well of his offerings.
- c) God didn't look with favor upon his offerings.
- d) God sent out fire to consume the offerings.

Pages 194–196   Pages 207–212   Pages 230–232   Pages 242–244

LEVEL 5

Of whom did Jesus say, "Among those born of women there has not risen anyone greater"?

 a) Paul
 b) Himself (Jesus)
 c) John the Baptist
 d) Lazarus

LEVEL 6

What nickname is sometimes applied to Fanny J. Crosby?

 a) Marching Matriarch
 b) Wizard of Menlo Park
 c) Swedish Nightingale
 d) Hymn Queen

LEVEL 7

What happened to the widow of Zarephath after she supplied Elijah with food?

 a) Her jar of flour was not used up, and the jug of oil did not run dry.
 b) She was invited to eat at the king's table.
 c) Twice as much was given to her.
 d) She was restored to health.

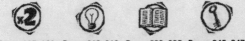

Pages 197–199   Pages 213–218   Pages 233–235   Pages 245–247

SILVER

In Albert E. Brumley's hymn "I'll Fly Away," where is his home located?

   a) "celestial shore"
   b) "green valley"
   c) "solid rock"
   d) "inside a crystal palace"

LEVEL 9

What did Elisha have to do to receive a double portion of Elijah's spirit?

   a) go upon a mountaintop to pray
   b) cross over Jordan and preach in the next village
   c) see Elijah as he was taken away
   d) build an altar on Mount Carmel

Pages 200–201   Pages 219–222   Pages 236–237   Pages 248–249

LEVEL 10

Albrecht Dürer's series of fifteen illustrations of the Apocalypse from Revelation was executed in what medium?

a) watercolor c) fresco
b) woodcut d) oil

LEVEL 11

What is the subtitle of Sojourner Truth's autobiography, *The Narrative of Sojourner Truth:…*?

a) *I Lay My Burden Down*
b) *A Northern Slave*
c) *The Autobiography of a Female Slave*
d) *Scenes in the Life*

GOLD

Who is called "the man of faith"?

a) Jacob c) Adam
b) Isaac d) Abraham

Pages 202–204 Pages 223–228 Pages 238–240 Pages 250–252

THIRTY INTERACTIVE QUIZZES THAT PUT YOU IN THE HOT SEAT

TRIVIA
FOR
LIFE

QUIZ 25

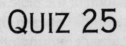
LEVEL 1

What practice of the church did Martin Luther oppose with his Ninety-five Theses?

 a) the doctrine of transubstantiation of the Lord's Supper
 b) the reliance upon tradition within the church
 c) buying indulgences (the release from the penalties of sin)
 d) the role of the pope

Page 193   Page 206   Page 229   Page 241

What two terms are associated with John Calvin's doctrine?

    a) works and faith
    b) conservatism and submission to authority
    c) election and predestination
    d) incarnation and atonement

For what is John Wycliffe noted?

    a) building the first English printing press
    b) first translation of the Bible into English
    c) urging a closer tie between church and state
    d) carrying Luther's reforms into England

BRONZE

What new believer did Barnabas introduce to the apostles in Jerusalem?

    a) the Ethiopian
    b) the jailer from Philippi
    c) Paul, then known as Saul
    d) Timothy

Pages 194–196 Pages 207–212 Pages 230–232 Pages 242–244

LEVEL 5

What did Brother Andrew (Andy van der Bijl) ask the Lord to do in his smuggler's prayer?

a) keep my car running
b) provide me a translator
c) put my foot in the door
d) make seeing eyes blind

LEVEL 6

What was the profession of Francis Scott Key, author of the United States national anthem?

a) lawyer
b) politician
c) sailor
d) businessman

LEVEL 7

How did Billy Sunday describe a response to the gospel call?

a) hitting the sawdust trail
b) sliding into home
c) reclaiming your birthright
d) receiving honey from the rock

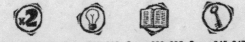

Pages 197–199   Pages 213–218   Pages 233–235   Pages 245–247

SILVER

What do the songs "Joy to the World" and "Jesus Shall Reign Wher'er the Sun" by Isaac Watts have in common?

    a) They were written after listening to sermons by John Calvin.

    b) Martin Luther wrote the music.

    c) Benjamin Franklin refused to publish them in America.

    d) They are based on psalms in the Bible.

LEVEL 9

When the children of Israel left slavery in Egypt, what happened to the bones of Joseph?

    a) Pharaoh ordered that they be burned and scattered.

    b) Moses took the bones with him.

    c) Pharaoh's daughter secretly buried them.

    d) They were lost forever.

Pages 200–201　Pages 219–222　Pages 236–237　Pages 248–249

LEVEL 10

What ministry did Dawson Trotman found?
- a) Youth with a Mission
- b) The Navigators
- c) Logos International
- d) World Wide Pictures

LEVEL 11

In addition to "kneel at the cross," what else does Charles E. Moody suggest in his song?
- a) "lay every burden down"
- b) "leave every care"
- c) "dwell in Beulah Land"
- d) "be covered with his blood"

GOLD

Where did William Tyndale begin printing his translation of the Bible?
- a) London, England
- b) Hague, The Netherlands
- c) Frankfurt, Germany
- d) Cologne, Germany

Pages 202–204   Pages 223–228   Pages 238–240   Pages 250–252

THIRTY INTERACTIVE QUIZZES THAT PUT YOU IN THE HOT SEAT

TRIVIA
FOR
LIFE

QUIZ 26

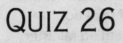

In the Stuart K. Hines translation of the Swedish folk melody "How Great Thou Art," after he sees the stars, what does he hear?

    a) "trumpet sound"
    b) "thunder"
    c) "whispering breezes"
    d) "unseen footsteps"

Page 193   Page 206   Page 229   Page 241

In the Isaac Watts song "When I Survey the Wondrous Cross," what is poured on "my pride"?

a) "generous love"
b) "sorrows"
c) "wings of faith"
d) "contempt"

For his work that began in Bristol, England, George Müller earned what title?

a) Poorest of the Poor
b) Bristol's Battling Minister
c) The Great Orator
d) Father of the Fatherless

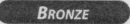

Mahalia Jackson is credited with bringing what music to a worldwide, multiracial audience?

a) ragtime   c) gospel
b) jazz   d) blues

Pages 194–196   Pages 207–212   Pages 230–232   Pages 242–244

LEVEL 5

Because of Ezra's wisdom of God, what was he expected to do?
- a) appoint magistrates and judges
- b) coordinate rebuilding the walls of Jerusalem
- c) make sure King Darius was happy
- d) supervise the distribution of land inheritance

LEVEL 6

Of what Scottish reformer did Mary, Queen of Scots, say, "I fear his prayers more than any army of ten thousand men"?
- a) George Wishart
- b) King James VI of Scotland
- c) Thomas Chalmers
- d) John Knox

LEVEL 7

Complete the title of the Isaac Watts song: "O God, Our Help in...."
- a) "Times of Distress"
- c) "Time of Need"
- b) "Ages Past"
- d) "Years to Come"

Pages 197–199   Pages 213–218   Pages 233–235   Pages 245–247

SILVER

Doctor C. Everett Koop collaborated with Francis Schaeffer on what book and film series?
- a) *The Flow of Biblical History*
- b) *A Christian Manifesto*
- c) *Whatever Happened to the Human Race?*
- d) *No Final Conflict*

LEVEL 9

Who was the pilot-missionary who died with Jim Elliot and the other missionaries in Ecuador?
- a) Nate Saint
- b) Johnny Angel
- c) Russell Pastor
- d) Reverend White

LEVEL 10

What did Mary the mother of Jesus do after He ascended into heaven?
- a) revisited the tomb where He was buried
- b) went for a walk in the Garden of Gethsemane
- c) went home to weep alone
- d) went to an upstairs room with many others

Pages 200–202   Pages 219–224   Pages 236–238   Pages 248–250

LEVEL 11

Which statement did William Tyndale make?
- a) "The plowboy will know the Scriptures better than the priests."
- b) "It is impossible that any word of man should be equal with Holy Scriptures."
- c) "We ought to believe in the authority of no man unless he says the word of God."
- d) "You get the language from the common man in the marketplace."

GOLD

Maltbie D. Babcock began his walks in the woods with what statement that later inspired a song?
- a) "I'm going out to see my Father's world."
- b) "I'm nearer home than I was yesterday."
- c) "I'm stepping in the light."
- d) "The path is long and steep."

Pages 203–204   Pages 225–228   Pages 239–240   Pages 251–252

THIRTY INTERACTIVE QUIZZES THAT PUT YOU IN THE HOT SEAT

TRIVIA
FOR
LIFE

QUIZ 27

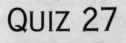

LEVEL 1

What did George Bennard describe as "rugged" in his song?

- a) a hillside
- b) a ship of state
- c) an old cross
- d) the road to Jericho

Page 193   Page 206   Page 229   Page 241

LEVEL 2

In his song, what did William Williams ask "Thou great Jehovah" to do?

    a) "hide me"   c) "guide me"
    b) "comfort me"   d) "show me"

LEVEL 3

What is the first phrase in the song "He Touched Me" by William J. Gaither?

    a) "Shackled by a heavy burden"
    b) "There is strength"
    c) "But praise God I belong"
    d) "Come, Holy Spirit"

BRONZE

The first stanza of the song "Silent Night" by Josef Mohr ends with what line?

    a) "sleep in heavenly peace"
    b) "round yon virgin mother and child"
    c) "all is calm, all is bright"
    d) "holy Infant so tender and mild"

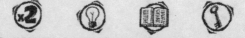

Pages 194–196   Pages 207–212   Pages 230–232   Pages 242–244

LEVEL 5

In the song "The Church in the Wildwood" by Dr. William S. Pitts, how does he describe the church?

a) "little brown church"
b) "log church"
c) "brick church"
d) "church with three bells"

LEVEL 6

What line is found in the song "Low in the Grave He Lay," by Robert Lowry?

a) "nothing can for sin atone"
b) "my feeble faith looks up"
c) "O bless me now, my Savior"
d) "He arose a victor from the dark domain"

LEVEL 7

Queen Esther risked her life by appearing unbidden before King Xerxes to press what worthy cause?

a) to remove the places of Baal worship
b) to prevent the killing of the Lord's prophets
c) to prevent the destruction of Jericho
d) to prevent the annihilation of the Jews

Pages 197–199 Pages 213–218 Pages 233–235 Pages 245–247

What career did Charles G. Finney leave to begin his Christian ministry?

- a) lawyer
- b) army officer
- c) ship's captain
- d) portrait painter

When the Church of England pulpits were closed to him, what did John Wesley describe as his parish?

- a) the Georgia Colony
- b) the poor
- c) the world
- d) Europe

LEVEL 10

Why did Charles Haddon Spurgeon withdraw from the Baptist Union?

- a) its increasingly liberal attitude
- b) it required a written examination to qualify for the ministry
- c) it insisted that he preach against evolution
- d) it refused to accept preachers of other denominations

Pages 200–202   Pages 219–224   Pages 236–238   Pages 248–250

LEVEL 11

In Joseph Medlicott Scriven's song that has the words "all our sins and griefs to bear," how does he describe Jesus?

a) king

c) friend

b) lover

d) fortress

GOLD

Why did Isaac Watts choose not to attend the University of Cambridge or Oxford?

a) He was so shy he could not leave home.

b) His grades were too poor.

c) He could not pay the tuition.

d) He was a Dissenter (Nonconformist).

Pages 203–204   Pages 225–228   Pages 239–240   Pages 251–252

THIRTY INTERACTIVE QUIZZES THAT PUT YOU IN THE HOT SEAT

TRIVIA
FOR
LIFE

QUIZ 28

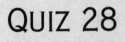

The 1611 authorized English translation of the Bible was named for what person?

a) James I of England
b) Edgar Johnson Goodspeed
c) William Tyndale
d) Edward de Vere, 17th earl of Oxford

Page 193   Page 206   Page 229   Page 241

LEVEL 2

The statement "Here I stand, I cannot do otherwise" is attributed to whom?

a) Joan of Arc   c) Galileo
b) Martin Luther   d) Copernicus

LEVEL 3

Although she repudiated it, what movie was based on the life of Gladys Aylward?

a) *China Diary*
b) *The Inn of the Sixth Happiness*
c) *The Sound of Music*
d) *The Good Earth*

BRONZE

What was David Livingstone's term for slave trading in Africa?

a) a stranger's treasure
b) the open sore of the world
c) perpetual despotism
d) peculiar institution

Pages 194–196   Pages 207–212   Pages 230–232   Pages 242–244

LEVEL 5

How does Gospel writer Luke describe
Theophilus?
  a) "Son of Encouragement"
  b) "a man after his own heart"
  c) "most excellent"
  d) "Rabbi"

LEVEL 6

How was Eunice related to Timothy?
  a) cousin
  b) sister
  c) grandmother
  d) mother

LEVEL 7

My Utmost for His Highest by Oswald Chambers
would best be described as what kind of book?
  a) historical novel
  b) religious allegory
  c) devotional book
  d) memoirs of a missionary

Pages 197–199   Pages 213–218   Pages 233–235   Pages 245–247

SILVER

Who was the Christian believer who discovered
the planet Uranus?
  a) William Herschel
  b) Ptolemy of Egypt
  c) Jonathan Edwards
  d) John Coach Adams

LEVEL 9

In the Bible, who was the first woman mentioned
by name after Eve?
  a) Naamah, Tubal-Cain's sister
  b) Adah, Lamech's wife
  c) Milcah, Nahor's wife
  d) Sarai or Sarah, Abraham's wife

LEVEL 10

The phrase "Teach me faith and duty" is from
which Philip P. Bliss song?
  a) "I Bring My Sins to Thee"
  b) "More Holiness Give Me"
  c) "Hallelujah! What a Savior!"
  d) "Wonderful Words of Life"

Pages 200–202   Pages 219–224   Pages 236–238   Pages 248–250

LEVEL 11

How did Sojourner Truth's family become free?
- a) as a result of the American Civil War
- b) by a law of 1828 that freed slaves in New York State
- c) by escaping to the North along the Underground Railroad
- d) by being set free by their "owner"

GOLD

What grandmother does Paul describe as having a sincere faith?
- a) Lois
- b) Eunice
- c) Tabitha
- d) Priscilla

Pages 203–204 Pages 225–228 Pages 239–240 Pages 251–252

THIRTY INTERACTIVE QUIZZES THAT PUT YOU IN THE HOT SEAT

TRIVIA
FOR
LIFE

QUIZ 29

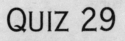

LEVEL 1

Paul is known as the apostle to what group?
  a) twelve tribes of Israel
  b) Hebrews
  c) Gentiles
  d) Macedonians

Page 193   Page 206   Page 229   Page 241

LEVEL 2

Who came to the empty tomb of Jesus while it was still dark?

    a) Mary Magdalene   c) Peter
    b) Herod   d) John

LEVEL 3

Noah was the first to see what phenomenon in the sky?

    a) shooting star
    b) rainbow
    c) northern lights
    d) comet

BRONZE

The words "And this be our motto, 'In God is our Trust'" are found in what song by Francis Scott Key?

    a) "Star Spangled Banner"
    b) "Hymn to the Flag"
    c) "Hymn of the Patriots"
    d) "God Save Our Beloved Country"

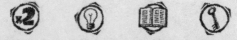

Pages 194–196   Pages 207–212   Pages 230–232   Pages 242–244

LEVEL 5

Teresa of Calcutta founded what organization?
- a) Sisters of Our Lady of Loreto
- b) Missionaries of Charity
- c) People of the Pure Heart
- d) City of Joy

LEVEL 6

What is a reasonable conclusion about
Onesimus in Paul's letter to Philemon?
- a) He was a runaway slave.
- b) He was an army deserter.
- c) He came from Caesar's household.
- d) He was a silversmith.

LEVEL 7

What South American tribe made martyrs of Jim
Elliot and four other missionary companions?
- a) Auca
- b) Carib
- c) Maya
- d) Tupi

Pages 197–199   Pages 213–218   Pages 233–235   Pages 245–247

In addition to Joseph, who was Rachel's other son?

    a) Levi   c) Reuben
    b) Benjamin   d) Dan

What is the third book of the *Perelandra* trilogy by C. S. Lewis?

    a) *Allegory of Love*
    b) *Out of the Silent Planet*
    c) *That Hideous Strength*
    d) *The Last Battle*

LEVEL 10

In his song when does Andraé Crouch say, "We are going to see the King?"

    a) "soon"
    b) "when the roll is called up yonder"
    c) "when the silver cord is broken"
    d) "at the end of life's way"

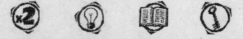

Pages 200–202   Pages 219–224   Pages 236–238   Pages 248–250

LEVEL 11

Henry Ward Beecher is noted primarily for which of his abilities?

    a) organizer of missions
    b) speaker
    c) songwriter
    d) writer

GOLD

What was the title of William Carey's pamphlet that began the Baptist Missionary Movement?

    a) *Enlarge the Place of Thy Tent*
    b) *Expect Great Things from God; Attempt Great Things for God*
    c) *Enquiry…to Use Means for the Conversion of the Heathens*
    d) *The Urgent Duty of the Missionary Society*

Pages 203–204   Pages 225–228   Pages 239–240   Pages 251–252

THIRTY INTERACTIVE QUIZZES THAT PUT YOU IN THE HOT SEAT

TRIVIA
FOR
LIFE

QUIZ 30

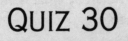

What advice did hymn writer Horatio R. Palmer make part of the title of his song about temptation?

  a) "pass over"
  b) "go right"
  c) "yield not"
  d) "turn around"

Page 193

Page 206

Page 229

Page 241

LEVEL 2

Jonathan Edwards is considered one of the evangelists who began what religious revival?

- a) Renaissance
- b) Protestant Reformation
- c) American Enlightenment
- d) Great Awakening

LEVEL 3

Although then known as separatists, Priscilla Mullins and the others aboard the *Mayflower* have become known by what name?

- a) Old Comers
- b) Leidenites
- c) Pilgrims
- d) Saints

BRONZE

How many times did Peter disown Jesus before the rooster crowed?

- a) two
- b) one
- c) twelve
- d) three

Pages 194–196   Pages 207–212   Pages 230–232   Pages 242–244

LEVEL 5

The song "Almost Persuaded" by Philip P. Bliss ends with what words?

 a) "I am saved by the blood of the crucified one."
 b) " 'Almost,' but lost!"
 c) "Grace hath redeemed us once for all."
 d) "Jesus loves even me."

LEVEL 6

Charles Haddon Spurgeon is noted for what aspect of his ministry?

 a) his efforts to reconcile Scripture and science
 b) his preaching
 c) his fund-raising
 d) his establishment of a worldwide evangelistic association

Pages 197–198   Pages 213–216   Pages 233–234   Pages 245–246

LEVEL 7

Hudson Taylor was the founder of what missionary organization?

    a) Interdenominational Foreign Mission
    b) China Inland Ministry
    c) Glad Tidings from England
    d) China's Spiritual Need

SILVER

Who was one of the prophets who appeared and
talked with Jesus when He was transfigured?

    a) Malachi   c) Elisha
    b) Gideon   d) Elijah

LEVEL 9

What phrase begins item 9 of the Dale Evans
and Roy Rogers Riders Club Rules: "Love God
and..."

    a) "always obey your parents."
    b) "go to Sunday school regularly."
    c) "be kind to animals."
    d) "consider others before yourself."

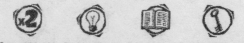

Pages 199–201 Pages 217–222 Pages 235–237 Pages 247–249

LEVEL 10

Where did Ruth Bell, wife of Billy Graham, spend her youth?

    a) Minneapolis, Minnesota
    b) China and Korea
    c) Montreat, North Carolina
    d) Wheaton, Illinois

LEVEL 11

Stephen's enemies hired men to say he had spoken against which Old Testament hero?

    a) Aaron   c) David
    b) Moses   d) Solomon

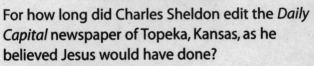

GOLD

For how long did Charles Sheldon edit the *Daily Capital* newspaper of Topeka, Kansas, as he believed Jesus would have done?

    a) one year
    b) one month
    c) one day
    d) one week

Pages 202–204   Pages 223–228   Pages 238–240   Pages 250–252

BONUSES

DOUBLE YOUR CHANCES

LEVEL 1

INCORRECT ANSWERS INCLUDE:

Quiz 1—B and D
Quiz 2—B and C
Quiz 3—A and D
Quiz 4—C and D
Quiz 5—B and C
Quiz 6—B and D
Quiz 7—B and D
Quiz 8—A and D
Quiz 9—B and D
Quiz 10—C and D
Quiz 11—A and C
Quiz 12—A and C
Quiz 13—C and D
Quiz 14—B and C
Quiz 15—B and C

Quiz 16—B and D
Quiz 17—A and B
Quiz 18—A and D
Quiz 19—A and C
Quiz 20—B and C
Quiz 21—B and D
Quiz 22—C and D
Quiz 23—A and B
Quiz 24—A and C
Quiz 25—A and D
Quiz 26—A and D
Quiz 27—A and D
Quiz 28—B and D
Quiz 29—A and D
Quiz 30—A and D

DOUBLE
YOUR CHANCES

LEVEL 2

INCORRECT ANSWERS INCLUDE:

Quiz 1—A and D

Quiz 2—A and C

Quiz 3—B and C

Quiz 4—A and D

Quiz 5—B and D

Quiz 6—B and D

Quiz 7—B and C

Quiz 8—C and D

Quiz 9—A and B

Quiz 10—A and D

Quiz 11—A and C

Quiz 12—A and D

Quiz 13—A and D

Quiz 14—A and D

Quiz 15—A and B

Quiz 16—B and D

Quiz 17—A and D

Quiz 18—A and D

Quiz 19—B and D

Quiz 20—A and B

Quiz 21—B and D

Quiz 22—B and D

Quiz 23—A and C

Quiz 24—A and B

Quiz 25—B and D

Quiz 26—A and C

Quiz 27—A and D

Quiz 28—A and D

Quiz 29—B and D

Quiz 30—B and C

DOUBLE YOUR CHANCES

LEVEL 3

INCORRECT ANSWERS INCLUDE:

Quiz 1—B and C

Quiz 2—C and D

Quiz 3—C and D

Quiz 4—A and B

Quiz 5—A and B

Quiz 6—C and D

Quiz 7—C and D

Quiz 8—B and C

Quiz 9—B and D

Quiz 10—A and D

Quiz 11—B and C

Quiz 12—B and D

Quiz 13—A and B

Quiz 14—A and B

Quiz 15—A and C

Quiz 16—A and D

Quiz 17—A and B

Quiz 18—C and D

Quiz 19—A and C

Quiz 20—B and D

Quiz 21—C and D

Quiz 22—B and C

Quiz 23—C and D

Quiz 24—A and B

Quiz 25—A and C

Quiz 26—A and B

Quiz 27—B and C

Quiz 28—A and C

Quiz 29—C and D

Quiz 30—A and B

DOUBLE YOUR CHANCES

BRONZE

INCORRECT ANSWERS INCLUDE:

Quiz 1—B and D	Quiz 16—A and C
Quiz 2—A and D	Quiz 17—B and C
Quiz 3—C and D	Quiz 18—C and D
Quiz 4—A and D	Quiz 19—A and D
Quiz 5—A and B	Quiz 20—A and B
Quiz 6—B and C	Quiz 21—B and C
Quiz 7—B and D	Quiz 22—C and D
Quiz 8—C and D	Quiz 23—A and D
Quiz 9—A and D	Quiz 24—A and C
Quiz 10—A and C	Quiz 25—A and B
Quiz 11—C and D	Quiz 26—B and D
Quiz 12—C and D	Quiz 27—C and D
Quiz 13—B and D	Quiz 28—C and D
Quiz 14—A and C	Quiz 29—B and C
Quiz 15—A and B	Quiz 30—A and B

DOUBLE YOUR CHANCES

LEVEL 5

INCORRECT ANSWERS INCLUDE:

Quiz 1—B and C

Quiz 2—A and C

Quiz 3—C and D

Quiz 4—A and B

Quiz 5—B and C

Quiz 6—B and D

Quiz 7—B and C

Quiz 8—C and D

Quiz 9—B and D

Quiz 10—B and D

Quiz 11—C and D

Quiz 12—B and C

Quiz 13—B and D

Quiz 14—A and D

Quiz 15—A and B

Quiz 16—A and B

Quiz 17—C and D

Quiz 18—A and D

Quiz 19—C and D

Quiz 20—A and C

Quiz 21—A and C

Quiz 22—B and D

Quiz 23—B and C

Quiz 24—B and D

Quiz 25—A and C

Quiz 26—C and D

Quiz 27—C and D

Quiz 28—A and D

Quiz 29—C and D

Quiz 30—C and D

198

DOUBLE YOUR CHANCES

LEVEL 6

INCORRECT ANSWERS INCLUDE:

Quiz 1—A and B

Quiz 2—C and D

Quiz 3—A and B

Quiz 4—A and C

Quiz 5—A and D

Quiz 6—B and D

Quiz 7—A and C

Quiz 8—C and D

Quiz 9—A and B

Quiz 10—C and D

Quiz 11—C and D

Quiz 12—A and C

Quiz 13—A and B

Quiz 14—A and C

Quiz 15—B and D

Quiz 16—B and C

Quiz 17—B and C

Quiz 18—B and C

Quiz 19—A and D

Quiz 20—A and B

Quiz 21—B and D

Quiz 22—A and B

Quiz 23—A and D

Quiz 24—A and B

Quiz 25—B and C

Quiz 26—B and C

Quiz 27—A and C

Quiz 28—B and C

Quiz 29—B and C

Quiz 30—C and D

DOUBLE YOUR CHANCES

LEVEL 7

INCORRECT ANSWERS INCLUDE:

Quiz 1—B and D

Quiz 2—A and B

Quiz 3—A and C

Quiz 4—A and C

Quiz 5—A and D

Quiz 6—A and C

Quiz 7—C and D

Quiz 8—B and D

Quiz 9—B and D

Quiz 10—B and C

Quiz 11—A and B

Quiz 12—A and B

Quiz 13—B and C

Quiz 14—A and C

Quiz 15—C and D

Quiz 16—B and D

Quiz 17—A and D

Quiz 18—C and D

Quiz 19—A and D

Quiz 20—A and C

Quiz 21—A and C

Quiz 22—A and C

Quiz 23—A and B

Quiz 24—B and D

Quiz 25—B and C

Quiz 26—C and D

Quiz 27—B and C

Quiz 28—B and D

Quiz 29—B and C

Quiz 30—C and D

DOUBLE YOUR CHANCES

SILVER

INCORRECT ANSWERS INCLUDE:

Quiz 1—C and D	Quiz 16—A and D
Quiz 2—C and D	Quiz 17—B and D
Quiz 3—C and D	Quiz 18—A and B
Quiz 4—A and B	Quiz 19—A and B
Quiz 5—B and C	Quiz 20—C and D
Quiz 6—B and C	Quiz 21—B and C
Quiz 7—A and D	Quiz 22—A and C
Quiz 8—C and D	Quiz 23—B and C
Quiz 9—C and D	Quiz 24—B and C
Quiz 10—A and D	Quiz 25—A and C
Quiz 11—A and C	Quiz 26—A and B
Quiz 12—A and D	Quiz 27—C and D
Quiz 13—A and C	Quiz 28—C and D
Quiz 14—A and D	Quiz 29—C and D
Quiz 15—B and D	Quiz 30—A and C

DOUBLE YOUR CHANCES

LEVEL 9

INCORRECT ANSWERS INCLUDE:

Quiz 1—B and C
Quiz 2—B and C
Quiz 3—C and D
Quiz 4—B and D
Quiz 5—B and D
Quiz 6—B and C
Quiz 7—B and C
Quiz 8—B and D
Quiz 9—A and C
Quiz 10—A and C
Quiz 11—A and C
Quiz 12—C and D
Quiz 13—A and B
Quiz 14—B and C
Quiz 15—A and D

Quiz 16—A and C
Quiz 17—A and C
Quiz 18—A and D
Quiz 19—A and C
Quiz 20—A and D
Quiz 21—C and D
Quiz 22—B and C
Quiz 23—A and C
Quiz 24—B and D
Quiz 25—A and D
Quiz 26—B and D
Quiz 27—A and B
Quiz 28—A and C
Quiz 29—B and D
Quiz 30—A and C

DOUBLE YOUR CHANCES

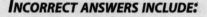

LEVEL 10

INCORRECT ANSWERS INCLUDE:

Quiz 1—B and D

Quiz 2—C and D

Quiz 3—B and C

Quiz 4—A and C

Quiz 5—B and D

Quiz 6—A and D

Quiz 7—A and C

Quiz 8—B and D

Quiz 9—C and D

Quiz 10—A and C

Quiz 11—C and D

Quiz 12—A and D

Quiz 13—C and D

Quiz 14—A and C

Quiz 15—A and B

Quiz 16—A and B

Quiz 17—B and D

Quiz 18—A and C

Quiz 19—C and D

Quiz 20—B and D

Quiz 21—B and C

Quiz 22—A and D

Quiz 23—A and C

Quiz 24—A and C

Quiz 25—C and D

Quiz 26—A and B

Quiz 27—B and C

Quiz 28—A and B

Quiz 29—B and C

Quiz 30—A and C

DOUBLE YOUR CHANCES

LEVEL 11

INCORRECT ANSWERS INCLUDE:

Quiz 1—B and D

Quiz 2—C and D

Quiz 3—A and C

Quiz 4—A and B

Quiz 5—C and D

Quiz 6—A and C

Quiz 7—A and B

Quiz 8—B and D

Quiz 9—B and C

Quiz 10—B and D

Quiz 11—A and B

Quiz 12—A and D

Quiz 13—A and C

Quiz 14—B and D

Quiz 15—B and D

Quiz 16—A and D

Quiz 17—B and D

Quiz 18—B and C

Quiz 19—A and C

Quiz 20—C and D

Quiz 21—A and C

Quiz 22—B and C

Quiz 23—A and B

Quiz 24—C and D

Quiz 25—A and D

Quiz 26—B and D

Quiz 27—A and B

Quiz 28—A and C

Quiz 29—A and D

Quiz 30—A and D

DOUBLE YOUR CHANCES

GOLD

INCORRECT ANSWERS INCLUDE:

Quiz 1—B and C	Quiz 16—C and D
Quiz 2—A and C	Quiz 17—B and C
Quiz 3—B and D	Quiz 18—A and D
Quiz 4—A and C	Quiz 19—B and C
Quiz 5—A and C	Quiz 20—A and C
Quiz 6—C and D	Quiz 21—A and C
Quiz 7—B and C	Quiz 22—A and B
Quiz 8—B and D	Quiz 23—B and D
Quiz 9—A and B	Quiz 24—B and C
Quiz 10—C and D	Quiz 25—A and C
Quiz 11—B and D	Quiz 26—B and D
Quiz 12—A and C	Quiz 27—A and C
Quiz 13—A and C	Quiz 28—B and C
Quiz 14—A and D	Quiz 29—B and D
Quiz 15—A and C	Quiz 30—A and B

HAVE A HINT

LEVEL 1

Quiz 1—Also known as the Book of Books.

Quiz 2—As in "_____ Bless America."

Quiz 3—A telephone you dial yourself without an operator.

Quiz 4—Short song, short name.

Quiz 5—Not a pellet of medication to be taken internally.

Quiz 6—Zero, zilch, nada, goose egg.

Quiz 7—A bookcase hid the entrance.

Quiz 8—For a special effect, mix red food color and syrup.

Quiz 9—Like Carl Sandburg's fog...

Quiz 10—Opposite the agony of defeat.

Quiz 11—Platform divers sometimes do only half of one.

Quiz 12—I don't know the words, but I can hum a few bars.

Quiz 13—Bermuda has a triangle and Wyoming has a tower.

Quiz 14—A visitor "not of this world."

Quiz 15—Think "from Stettin in the Baltic to Trieste in the Adriatic."

Quiz 16—Camouflaged to conceal an identity.

Quiz 17—Yellowstone's best-known geyser.

Quiz 18—But it's not about Ben Hur.

Quiz 19—The first three letters are a transgression of the Ten Commandments.

Quiz 20—Heroism ends with the same letters.

Quiz 21—Is it O positive or B negative?

Quiz 22—When change failed, opposition followed.

Quiz 23—Pronto...

Quiz 24—Subject of Lincoln's proclamation of 1863.

Quiz 25—Follow the money.

Quiz 26—Sound from a lightning discharge.

Quiz 27—You can do this to your fingers and your heart.

Quiz 28—He also had a "town" in Virginia.

Quiz 29—The word comes from "gentle."

Quiz 30—In both the United States and Europe, this traffic sign is triangular.

HAVE A HINT

LEVEL 2

Quiz 1—Hallelujah has the same meaning.

Quiz 2—A government worker: civil _____.

Quiz 3—In Arab countries, the flag has a scarlet crescent.

Quiz 4—Aaron could be described as "silver tongued."

Quiz 5—Originally, military expeditions to the Holy Land.

Quiz 6—Abraham Lincoln was born in one.

Quiz 7—What Columbus sought by sailing west.

Quiz 8—The EKG is not a flat line.

Quiz 9—Home of cheese and chocolate.

Quiz 10—Bracelets with the letters WWJD summarize the question.

Quiz 11—It has twenty-eight bones.

Quiz 12—It's a wind instrument.

Quiz 13—Without insects, life itself is impossible.

Quiz 14—Did he also name the projection at the front of your throat?

Quiz 15—George Washington could have said the same about Benedict Arnold.

Quiz 16—It's similar to the title of Dickens's book that begins "It was the best of times, it was the worse of times."

Quiz 17—She often made the final bed check of injured soldiers well after dark.

Quiz 18—The coronation of 1952 gave Great Britain a queen of the same name.

Quiz 19—What a gentleman offered a lady as she stepped from a coach.

Quiz 20—They sought a disciplined method of spiritual improvement.

Quiz 21—The name is Lucas in Latin.

Quiz 22—Short answer…

Quiz 23—An instrument to announce the arrival of a king.

Quiz 24—Think about the elderly Cuban in Hemingway's short novel.

Quiz 25—The first Tuesday after the first Monday in November in the United States.

Quiz 26—Disrespect in court …

Quiz 27—A Seeing Eye dog."

Quiz 28—Comic duo Dean _____ and Jerry Lewis.

Quiz 29—M & M, but not candy.

Quiz 30—What bears do in spring.

HAVE
A HINT

LEVEL 3

Quiz 1—The first name of the president from Quincy, Massachusetts.

Quiz 2—Moisture-laden fragrant flowers with prickly stems.

Quiz 3—Because of the height, it took an "angel" to paint it.

Quiz 4—The eatable parts grow underground.

Quiz 5—"Walk a mile in them…"

Quiz 6—Look before you leap…

Quiz 7—The fourth Thursday in November.

Quiz 8—Native American Nez Percé leader Chief ____.

Quiz 9—It would take a maternity maturity ward.

Quiz 10—Reach out and ____ somebody.

Quiz 11—Neither fig nor Wayne.

Quiz 12—The U.S. Navy's military police are known as the ____ patrol.

Quiz 13—Its official publication is "The War Cry."

Quiz 14—Think carpus and phalanges.

Quiz 15—Splendor to the infant monarch.

Quiz 16—A female parent.

Quiz 17—Take the first letter of Jesus, others, yourself.

Quiz 18—Charles Dickens's character: _____ Copperfield.

Quiz 19—Knights wore shining metallic suits.

Quiz 20—He wore white socks in Chicago.

Quiz 21—A twining vine: the _____ glory.

Quiz 22—What would Johnny Appleseed sing about?

Quiz 23—He showed Goliath his skill with a slingshot.

Quiz 24—Columbus named Native Americans for this destination.

Quiz 25—Two hundred years before the King James Version.

Quiz 26—More than genes are required to be one.

Quiz 27—How Harry Houdini was restrained.

Quiz 28—The number was reduced from eight.

Quiz 29—Roy G Biv tells the order of the colors.

Quiz 30—John Wayne: "Well, listen, _____."

HAVE A HINT

BRONZE

Quiz 1—John Philip Sousa music.

Quiz 2—A fraternal question.

Quiz 3—One of Satan's henchmen for each of the seven deadly sins.

Quiz 4—Think double w.

Quiz 5—Did they change color in the fall?

Quiz 6—Jesus spoke the beatitudes from such a location.

Quiz 7—Six-foot six-inch basketball player Michael .

Quiz 8—A tourniquet stems the flow.

Quiz 9—CPR for the soul.

Quiz 10—We try to keep these; He is certain to.

Quiz 11—A global worry…

Quiz 12—Usually portrayed as a limbless reptile.

Quiz 13—Fungi can do without it.

Quiz 14—If Peter had a sister, so would Andrew.

Quiz 15—Homer and Milton would have been in good company with her.

Quiz 16—Little Bo Peep had a similar occupation.

Quiz 17—Antique enemy...

Quiz 18—Judy Garland's St. Louis World's Fair movie.

Quiz 19—Vertigo...

Quiz 20—George Orwell's *Animal Farm* is one of the few modern examples.

Quiz 21—You'd find one in a Brinks armored truck.

Quiz 22—A place for clothes.

Quiz 23—SOS would be appropriate.

Quiz 24—Abel got an "atta boy."

Quiz 25—Did he suggest the name change?

Quiz 26—Jerry Falwell's television broadcast, the "Old Time _____ Hour."

Quiz 27—A newborn does it for about 16 hours a day.

Quiz 28—Unobstructed skin lesion of the human habitation.

Quiz 29—He wrote it by the rockets' red glare.

Quiz 30—Subtract four from the number of days in the week.

HAVE A HINT

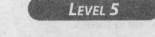
LEVEL 5

Quiz 1—Alms for the poor.

Quiz 2—He prevented Southern forces from capturing Washington, D.C., during the Civil War.

Quiz 3—They have trumpet-shaped flowers.

Quiz 4—They were sad, you see.

Quiz 5—Don't tell the NFL.

Quiz 6—The name rhymes with macaroni.

Quiz 7—The family name would survive.

Quiz 8—A dove carrying an olive branch...

Quiz 9—The original Nick at Nite.

Quiz 10—The Charge of the Light Brigade was a "crime."

Quiz 11—He had a lot of time on his hands.

Quiz 12—According to Noel Coward, only mad dogs and Englishmen go out in its noonday sun.

Quiz 13—London's West End manors had these both upstairs and downstairs.

Quiz 14—Soldiers met in battle wearing blue and gray.

Quiz 15—The only one known by three names.

Quiz 16—Vegetarians need not apply.

Quiz 17—They are usually shown with wings and a harp.

Quiz 18—Pronounce his name differently for a task to be done.

Quiz 19—Good things come in threes.

Quiz 20—The inscription on his crypt in a church reads, "If you seek his monument, look around."

Quiz 21—He engaged his little gray cells.

Quiz 22—Back to basics...

Quiz 23—Anagram: Daily.

Quiz 24—Attila the Hun and Peter the Great had the same middle name.

Quiz 25—Like a guide dog with a white cane.

Quiz 26—They have power to enforce the law.

Quiz 27—A drab color.

Quiz 28—Equivalent to a grade of A plus.

Quiz 29—It follows Lincoln's statement that begins "with malice toward none, ..."

Quiz 30—Only in horseshoes can falling short count.

HAVE A HINT

LEVEL 6

Quiz 1—The Nile runs through it.

Quiz 2—Two pairs of double letters.

Quiz 3—One was the child of the other's uncle.

Quiz 4—Number of islands in the salad dressing.

Quiz 5—She was taking a "bath" when David saw her.

Quiz 6—The same complaint is made of drivers who use cell phones.

Quiz 7—He wrote a book defending writing in the vernacular.

Quiz 8—He needed skill at the first of the three Rs.

Quiz 9—Sounds like water at 212 degrees Fahrenheit.

Quiz 10—Ships would prefer it during stormy weather.

Quiz 11—Think "good" about a citizen from there.

Quiz 12—He developed the process to keep milk from spoiling.

Quiz 13—If the meaning of her name matched her disposition, she had a rosy outlook.

Quiz 14—When he did, Jesus gained another disciple.

Quiz 15—No strings attached...

Quiz 16—His enemies wanted him dead, dead.

Quiz 17—Consider Robert Stroud's feathered subjects of study at Alcatraz.

Quiz 18—His given name is the same as Princess Diana's oldest son.

Quiz 19—Consider the third inalienable right of the Declaration of Independence.

Quiz 20—Batteries not included.

Quiz 21—Last words are the title to the Beatles' last album.

Quiz 22—It's not the gift but the thought that counts.

Quiz 23—A new name after being "born again."

Quiz 24—She wrote about 6,000 songbook entries.

Quiz 25—Dick the butcher of Shakespeare's *Henry VI*: "First you kill the _____."

Quiz 26—Append "ville" for a city in Tennessee.

Quiz 27—Opposite of the agony of defeat.

Quiz 28—Today, he would telephone her on the second Sunday in May.

Quiz 29—No Underground Railroad for him.

Quiz 30—His sermons filled 50 volumes.

HAVE A HINT

LEVEL 7

Quiz 1—An "old-fashioned gospel" preacher.

Quiz 2—When she died, the destitute missed her.

Quiz 3—Think Demosthenes and Daniel Webster.

Quiz 4—The wrong name on the wanted poster.

Quiz 5—What a hospice volunteer does.

Quiz 6—Where the ball goes when the announcer says, "He shoots, he scores!"

Quiz 7—Always the paperwork...

Quiz 8—Roget would say the "municipality of ruin."

Quiz 9—They warn of treacherous coastal waters.

Quiz 10—The people of Plymouth Colony.

Quiz 11—Espionage is not for the faint of heart.

Quiz 12—The original "hush puppy" food.

Quiz 13—Last word is decorative iron.

Quiz 14—He began at the beginning.

Quiz 15—Charlton Heston parted the Red Sea in this role.

Quiz 16—Opposite of a dirty devil.

Quiz 17—A major city together with its suburbs.

Quiz 18—Think days ahead and times before.

Quiz 19—Words of single syllables.

Quiz 20—Pioneer television comic _____ Berle.

Quiz 21—Often quoted as "give," Nathan Hale instead used this word in his last statement.

Quiz 22—Steven Spielberg's movie with Oprah Winfrey had the same color in the title.

Quiz 23—She was probably from the town of Magdala.

Quiz 24—The original "all you care to eat" buffet.

Quiz 25—Was it a "beaten" path?

Quiz 26—It's the time frame of archaeology.

Quiz 27—A BC holocaust in the making.

Quiz 28—Take a daily vitamin for the human spirit.

Quiz 29—The first alphabetically.

Quiz 30—In case of a typhoon, it's a good location.

HAVE A HINT

SILVER

Quiz 1—Fingertips to fingertips...

Quiz 2—Hydrotherapy...

Quiz 3—His price was twenty shekels of silver.

Quiz 4—The number of angles in a triangle.

Quiz 5—A highly contagious disease.

Quiz 6—The germ killer Listerine was named in his honor.

Quiz 7—To be politically correct, person.

Quiz 8—Marco Polo saw this practice that gave Chinese women dainty appearances.

Quiz 9—Pulp and historical are cousins of this genre.

Quiz 10—Columbus's flagship carried the same name.

Quiz 11—But Paul was bound and determined to go to Jerusalem.

Quiz 12—Henry Morton Stanley said, "Dr. ____, I presume."

Quiz 13—She had four times the experience of a twenty-one year old.

Quiz 14—The watcher was a female sibling.

Quiz 15—A whodunit…

Quiz 16—He traveled with a container of bread and fruit of the vine.

Quiz 17—Think generous patrons…

Quiz 18—Meet one in an ER…

Quiz 19—I'm all ears.

Quiz 20—When opportunity knocks, let it in.

Quiz 21—William Clark's partner in the "Corps of Discovery."

Quiz 22—Greyfriars Bobby, the dog, had this attribute.

Quiz 23—Did the homeowner's insurance repair the damage?

Quiz 24—A heavenly beach.

Quiz 25—Paraphrased Scripture.

Quiz 26—They were not talking about the 100m dash.

Quiz 27—Marshall Matt Dillon brought _____ and order to Dodge City.

Quiz 28—Last name begins with feminine pronoun.

Quiz 29—The first name of the American who flew a kite during a lightning storm.

Quiz 30—Every other letter is a vowel.

HAVE A HINT

LEVEL 9

Quiz 1—Could their fleece be white as snow?

Quiz 2—As a youth, Whitefield had been interested in acting and theater.

Quiz 3—"We shall overcome" for females.

Quiz 4—The reason Jack and Jill went up the hill.

Quiz 5—The buddy system.

Quiz 6—Shorthand came in handy.

Quiz 7—A quarter of a year.

Quiz 8—Squash begins with the letters of the name.

Quiz 9—To sketch with a pencil.

Quiz 10—Jefferson's land deal, the Louisiana _____.

Quiz 11—"___ is believing."

Quiz 12—He wore a queue.

Quiz 13—The Gestapo tried to force Bonhoeffer to _____ crimes against Hitler.

Quiz 14—The first name of Simon who met the pie man.

Quiz 15—The wrong kind puffeth up.

Quiz 16—It means a petition.

Quiz 17—It is more than the absence of war.

Quiz 18—Although in his day the term "Indians" was used.

Quiz 19—She was a judge and ruled Israel.

Quiz 20—Vegetables would grow there, too.

Quiz 21—Later, he completed the studies and took the Hippocratic oath.

Quiz 22—And it wasn't even the third Sunday in June.

Quiz 23—The only one with "spirit."

Quiz 24—He needed the motto of the Pinkertons: We never sleep.

Quiz 25—They crossed the Red Sea, too.

Quiz 26—Think rhyming...

Quiz 27—The 1900s had two wars named after the correct choice.

Quiz 28—After adage and before Adam in the dictionary.

Quiz 29—The Olympic event "clean and jerk" requires this.

Quiz 30—Dress in your best...

HAVE A HINT

Quiz 1—Canada geese migrate more quickly with its help.

Quiz 2—The sun does it each morning.

Quiz 3—For Bonhoeffer it became the cost of living.

Quiz 4—Native American moon...

Quiz 5—Participants do this in the Olympic marathon.

Quiz 6—Consider his wife's first name: Joy.

Quiz 7—It wasn't because of a migraine.

Quiz 8—No need to carry credit cards.

Quiz 9—First word is a woman's name.

Quiz 10—Reading and 'riting and 'rithmetic...

Quiz 11—A college professor has a similar job.

Quiz 12—He couldn't sleep or concentrate; he felt sad.

Quiz 13—He said "aye, aye, sir" to God.

Quiz 14—What happens when a long and boring sermon ends.

Quiz 15—The flower _____'s Ladder is named for one of his dreams.

Quiz 16—Think divine blueprints.

Quiz 17—The female of the species.

Quiz 18—Cartoon, a boy and his tiger: "_____ and Hobbs."

Quiz 19—A believer's alias.

Quiz 20—Ends with morning network TV news show...

Quiz 21—The ending "g" is dropped.

Quiz 22—Like Bob Barker, he said, "Come on down!"

Quiz 23—It is a percussion instrument.

Quiz 24—Extra copies were "a chip off the old block."

Quiz 25—Compass and sextant...

Quiz 26—She did not have an elevator to get there.

Quiz 27—A college degree for a nonscientist is called a _____ arts degree.

Quiz 28—It shares words with the Jimmy Stewart classic Christmas movie: *It's a* _____ _____.

Quiz 29—Participants in the Oklahoma Land Rush...

Quiz 30—Home of the Great Wall.

HAVE A HINT

LEVEL 11

Quiz 1—The number of strikes in an out.

Quiz 2—Brothers told him to "Go west, young man."

Quiz 3—A young man of great physical beauty?

Quiz 4—A generous titan of industry.

Quiz 5—They could say, "Here comes the judge!"

Quiz 6—Hans Anderson's middle name.

Quiz 7—Life insurance companies could not do without it.

Quiz 8—The umpire calls the ball "low and _____."

Quiz 9—Her first name is the city of her birth in this country.

Quiz 10—A word that is used to ask permission of a court.

Quiz 11—Ends with the worldwide staple cereal grain.

Quiz 12—A Sanskrit version of the Rosetta stone would have helped.

Quiz 13—Look for the "no" in the middle of the name.

Quiz 14—Preacher to the Western Hemisphere south of the United States.

Quiz 15—The material world...

Quiz 16—Life, liberty and the _____ of happiness.

Quiz 17—Consider Bobbie Gentry's song "_____ Valley PTA."

Quiz 18—A hilarious joke should earn the same response.

Quiz 19—You can't take the pass book with you.

Quiz 20—Tissues are advertised as having this property.

Quiz 21—A cookie named after Newton.

Quiz 22—Former President Clinton's hometown in Arkansas.

Quiz 23—She was barren and beyond childbearing years.

Quiz 24—A slave on the New York side of the Mason-Dixon Line.

Quiz 25—Abandon worries without exception.

Quiz 26—He would be turning over the soil in the spring.

Quiz 27—A Quaker might agree.

Quiz 28—The state acted before the federal government.

Quiz 29—Patrick Henry and William Jennings Bryan also held people's attention with this skill.

Quiz 30—Often portrayed holding two stone tablets.

HAVE
A HINT

GOLD

Quiz 1—To play the role in a movie, women need not apply.

Quiz 2—Phototropic plants do it when the sun is overhead.

Quiz 3—She was known as Amma, meaning "mother" in the Tamil language.

Quiz 4—Countryman to Sir Walter Scott and Robert Louis Stevenson.

Quiz 5—Shares a name with the scientist Asimov.

Quiz 6—Romulus and Remus, Castor and Pollux, . . .

Quiz 7—Although it is not likely that she was led around by it.

Quiz 8—The planet Venus is also known by this name.

Quiz 9—Migrating Canada geese do it.

Quiz 10—He is not related to the big-band leader.

Quiz 11—Not the coffee.

Quiz 12—A victim of Hitler's executioners.

Quiz 13—A place to stay during an alpine blizzard.

Quiz 14—Despite coming up from bondage, he wrote with eloquence and brilliance.

Quiz 15—And they were not referring to the black clover of a playing card.

Quiz 16—The thrill of victory...

Quiz 17—Who could find first name "Brother" last name "Andrew"?

Quiz 18—Also known as a domestic.

Quiz 19—Probably not the result of a potato fungus.

Quiz 20—Gaggle and pride are similar names.

Quiz 21—In English, his last name means to remove with a knife.

Quiz 22—He arranged pony rides and picnics for them.

Quiz 23—A contraction of "am not."

Quiz 24—The 16th U. S. president's first name.

Quiz 25—Also the home of the men's fragrance.

Quiz 26—God's terrestrial sphere.

Quiz 27—A minority opinion...

Quiz 28—There is no "t" in this name.

Quiz 29—Those who did not acknowledge the God of Abraham.

Quiz 30—Seven days without God makes one weak.

LOOK IN THE BOOK

LEVEL 1

LOOK IN THE BOOK

LEVEL 2

Quiz 1—Romans 15:11

Quiz 2—Luke 1:38

Quiz 3—Colossians 1:20

Quiz 4—Exodus 4:14–16

Quiz 5—Mark 15:13 begins with first three letters

Quiz 6—1 Chronicles 27:32

Quiz 7—Mark 16:1

Quiz 8—John 14:19

Quiz 9—Matthew 27:45 ends with last word

Quiz 10—Mark 10:51

Quiz 11—Acts 7:50

Quiz 12—1 Thessalonians 4:16

Quiz 13—Matthew 3:4

Quiz 14—Genesis 2:19

Quiz 15—Mark 14:18

Quiz 16—Mark 1:1

Quiz 17—Mark 4:21

Quiz 18—Luke 1:24

Quiz 19—Psalm 18:35

Quiz 20—Ruth 4:7

Quiz 21—Colossians 4:14

Quiz 22—Ephesians 4:11

Quiz 23—Matthew 24:31

Quiz 24—Matthew 4:19

Quiz 25—2 Peter 1:10

Quiz 26—1 Thessalonians 5:20

Quiz 27—Psalm 43:3

Quiz 28—Revelation 3:16 word five first two letters + word six last four letters

Quiz 29—John 20:1

Quiz 30—Isaiah 52:1

LOOK IN THE BOOK

LEVEL 3

LOOK IN
THE BOOK

BRONZE

Quiz 1—1 Peter 2:6

Quiz 2—Genesis 4:9

Quiz 3—Mark 16:9

Quiz 4—John 5:17

Quiz 5—Genesis 3:7

Quiz 6—Isaiah 13:2

Quiz 7—Matthew 3:5

Quiz 8—Mark 10:45

Quiz 9—Psalm 85:6

Quiz 10—Psalm 106:12

Quiz 11—Genesis 11:1

Quiz 12—Genesis 3:15

Quiz 13—Job 8:16

Quiz 14—John 1:40

Quiz 15—Acts 9:9

Quiz 16—Genesis 4:2

Quiz 17—Psalm 61:3

Quiz 18—2 Kings 6:1

Quiz 19—Acts 19:32

Quiz 20—Ezekiel 17:2

Quiz 21—John 13:29

Quiz 22—Proverbs 30:30

Quiz 23—Psalm 69:18

Quiz 24—Hebrews 11:4

Quiz 25—Acts 9:27

Quiz 26—Mark 13:10

Quiz 27—Psalm 4:8

Quiz 28—Isaiah 1:6

Quiz 29—Matthew 2:10

Quiz 30—Matthew 26:75

LOOK IN THE BOOK

LEVEL 5

Quiz 1—Mark 10:46

Quiz 2—Mark 6:21

Quiz 3—Matthew 6:28

Quiz 4—Matthew 3:7

Quiz 5—Acts 20:7

Quiz 6—Ruth 1:15–16

Quiz 7—Luke 7:15

Quiz 8—Jude 1:2

Quiz 9—John 3:1–2

Quiz 10—2 Samuel 8:6

Quiz 11—Acts 5:18

Quiz 12—Esther 1:1

Quiz 13—Psalm 123:2

Quiz 14—2 Timothy 2:4

Quiz 15—Luke 13:34 first four letters of last word

Quiz 16—Acts 10:12–13

Quiz 17—Acts 27:23

Quiz 18—Job 1:8

Quiz 19—Deuteronomy 19:9

Quiz 20—Hebrews 11:10

Quiz 21—1 Corinthians 3:20

Quiz 22—Acts 2:13 fourth word begins correct answer

Quiz 23—Acts 16:14

Quiz 24—Matthew 11:11

Quiz 25—John 12:40

Quiz 26—Ezra 7:25

Quiz 27—Zechariah 1:8

Quiz 28—Luke 1:3

Quiz 29—1 Corinthians 13:13 (KJV)

Quiz 30—Psalm 73:2

234

LOOK IN THE BOOK

LEVEL 6

LOOK IN THE BOOK

LEVEL 7

LOOK IN
THE BOOK

SILVER

Quiz 1—1 Timothy 2:8
Quiz 2—Psalm 42:1
Quiz 3—Genesis 37:28
Quiz 4—Genesis 4:25
Quiz 5—Deuteronomy
25:14 last word
Quiz 6—Acts 11:27 starts
with letters of last
word
Quiz 7—1 Corinthians 2:15
Quiz 8—Luke 7:46
Quiz 9—1 Thessalonians
1:3
Quiz 10—Acts 27:6
Quiz 11—Acts 21:11
Quiz 12—1 Peter 2:5
words four and five
Quiz 13—Luke 2:37
Quiz 14—Exodus 2:4
Quiz 15—Ephesians 5:32

Quiz 16—1 Corinthians
11:20
Quiz 17—Luke 8:1–3
Quiz 18—Jeremiah 8:22
Quiz 19—1 Samuel 3:10
Quiz 20—Colossians 4:3
Quiz 21—1 Peter 5:4
initials of words four
and five
Quiz 22—Philippians 4:3
Quiz 23—Mark 2:4
Quiz 24—Luke 5:11
Quiz 25—Psalm 98:1
Quiz 26—1 Corinthians
9:8
Quiz 27—Titus 3:13
Quiz 28—Genesis 12:3
starts with second
word
Quiz 29—Genesis 35:24
Quiz 30—Matthew 17:3

LOOK IN THE BOOK

LEVEL 9

Quiz 1—Genesis 29:9
Quiz 2—Matthew 10:20
Quiz 3—Psalm 45:9
Quiz 4—Genesis 24:15
Quiz 5—Acts 19:29
Quiz 6—John 9:34
Quiz 7—Hebrews 11:23
Quiz 8—Luke 15:13 first five letters of longest word
Quiz 9—Hebrews 7:19
Quiz 10—Proverbs 20:14
Quiz 11—John 1:46
Quiz 12—Luke 20:39
Quiz 13—Philippians 2:11
Quiz 14—1 Timothy 2:7

Quiz 15—Acts 18:24
Quiz 16—1 Samuel 1:20
Quiz 17—Judges 6:24
Quiz 18—Acts 18:24
Quiz 19—Judges 4:4
Quiz 20—1 Kings 21:7
Quiz 21—Proverbs 17:22
Quiz 22—Genesis 29:12
Quiz 23—Ephesians 5:19
Quiz 24—2 Kings 2:9-10
Quiz 25—Exodus 13:19
Quiz 26—Psalm 116:15
Quiz 27—Matthew 5:14
Quiz 28—Genesis 4:19
Quiz 29—Philippians 4:13
Quiz 30—Acts 10:2 last word

238

Look in
the Book

LEVEL 10

Quiz 1—Proverbs 25:23
Quiz 2—John 11:23
Quiz 3—Luke 14:27
Quiz 4—Luke 1:26
Quiz 5—Acts 8:30
Quiz 6—John 3:7
Quiz 7—Luke 14:2
Quiz 8—Romans 13:8
Quiz 9—Isaiah 43:26
Quiz 10—Job 36:22
Quiz 11—Ezra 7:10
Quiz 12—1 Samuel 16:23
Quiz 13—2 Kings 18:5–6
Quiz 14—Psalm 57:8
Quiz 15—John 4:6
Quiz 16—Hebrews 11:10
Quiz 17—John 4:9; 4:29
Quiz 18—Matthew 11:18

Quiz 19—Isaiah 62:2
Quiz 20—Matthew 28:6
Quiz 21—Matthew 13:53
Quiz 22—1 Timothy 4:13
Quiz 23—Exodus 15:20
Quiz 24—Deuteronomy 19:5
Quiz 25—Genesis 2:14 first five letters begins correct answer
Quiz 26—Acts 1:13–14
Quiz 27—Philippians 2:5
Quiz 28—John 6:63
Quiz 29—Revelation 22:20
Quiz 30—Leviticus 13:29 begins with last word

LOOK IN THE BOOK

LEVEL 11

Quiz 1—Exodus 7:7
Quiz 2—Luke 1:60
Quiz 3—Acts 18:24–26
Quiz 4—Leviticus 27:30
Quiz 5—Job 9:33
Quiz 6—1 Peter 4:16
Quiz 7—Deuteronomy 1:12
Quiz 8—John 11:20
Quiz 9—Hebrews 13:24
Quiz 10—Hebrews 11:5
Quiz 11—Acts 26:30 (similar)
Quiz 12—Ezra 4:18
Quiz 13—Hebrews 11:5
Quiz 14—John 19:20
Quiz 15—1 Corinthians 11:14

Quiz 16—2 Samuel 2:27
Quiz 17—2 Samuel 3:22
Quiz 18—Genesis 17:17
Quiz 19—Proverbs 23:14
Quiz 20—Psalm 65:10 first four letters of word 10
Quiz 21—Amos 7:14
Quiz 22—Ephesians 4:4
Quiz 23—Luke 1:36–37
Quiz 24—Job 26:7
Quiz 25—Matthew 15:14
Quiz 26—Luke 9:62
Quiz 27—Luke 5:20
Quiz 28—Jeremiah 34:10
Quiz 29—Acts 14:12
Quiz 30—Acts 6:11

LOOK IN THE BOOK

GOLD

ANSWERS

LEVEL 1

Quiz 1—C	Quiz 16—C
Quiz 2—A	Quiz 17—D
Quiz 3—B	Quiz 18—C
Quiz 4—A	Quiz 19—D
Quiz 5—A	Quiz 20—A
Quiz 6—A	Quiz 21—A
Quiz 7—A	Quiz 22—A
Quiz 8—C	Quiz 23—C
Quiz 9—A	Quiz 24—D
Quiz 10—B	Quiz 25—C
Quiz 11—D	Quiz 26—B
Quiz 12—B	Quiz 27—C
Quiz 13—A	Quiz 28—A
Quiz 14—A	Quiz 29—C
Quiz 15—A	Quiz 30—C

ANSWERS

LEVEL 2

Quiz 1—B
Quiz 2—B
Quiz 3—D
Quiz 4—B
Quiz 5—C
Quiz 6—C
Quiz 7—A
Quiz 8—B
Quiz 9—D
Quiz 10—C
Quiz 11—B
Quiz 12—C
Quiz 13—C
Quiz 14—B
Quiz 15—D

Quiz 16—A
Quiz 17—C
Quiz 18—C
Quiz 19—C
Quiz 20—D
Quiz 21—C
Quiz 22—C
Quiz 23—D
Quiz 24—D
Quiz 25—C
Quiz 26—D
Quiz 27—C
Quiz 28—B
Quiz 29—A
Quiz 30—D

ANSWERS

LEVEL 3

Quiz 1—D	Quiz 16—C
Quiz 2—B	Quiz 17—D
Quiz 3—A	Quiz 18—B
Quiz 4—D	Quiz 19—D
Quiz 5—C	Quiz 20—A
Quiz 6—B	Quiz 21—B
Quiz 7—B	Quiz 22—A
Quiz 8—D	Quiz 23—A
Quiz 9—C	Quiz 24—C
Quiz 10—B	Quiz 25—B
Quiz 11—A	Quiz 26—D
Quiz 12—A	Quiz 27—A
Quiz 13—D	Quiz 28—B
Quiz 14—C	Quiz 29—B
Quiz 15—D	Quiz 30—C

ANSWERS

BRONZE

Quiz 1—C	Quiz 16—D
Quiz 2—B	Quiz 17—A
Quiz 3—B	Quiz 18—B
Quiz 4—B	Quiz 19—B
Quiz 5—C	Quiz 20—D
Quiz 6—A	Quiz 21—A
Quiz 7—C	Quiz 22—B
Quiz 8—B	Quiz 23—C
Quiz 9—C	Quiz 24—B
Quiz 10—B	Quiz 25—C
Quiz 11—B	Quiz 26—C
Quiz 12—A	Quiz 27—A
Quiz 13—C	Quiz 28—B
Quiz 14—D	Quiz 29—A
Quiz 15—D	Quiz 30—D

ANSWERS

LEVEL 5

Quiz 1—A	Quiz 16—D
Quiz 2—D	Quiz 17—B
Quiz 3—B	Quiz 18—C
Quiz 4—C	Quiz 19—A
Quiz 5—D	Quiz 20—D
Quiz 6—C	Quiz 21—B
Quiz 7—D	Quiz 22—C
Quiz 8—A	Quiz 23—D
Quiz 9—C	Quiz 24—C
Quiz 10—A	Quiz 25—D
Quiz 11—B	Quiz 26—A
Quiz 12—A	Quiz 27—A
Quiz 13—C	Quiz 28—C
Quiz 14—B	Quiz 29—B
Quiz 15—D	Quiz 30—B

ANSWERS

LEVEL 6

Quiz 1—D	Quiz 16—A
Quiz 2—A	Quiz 17—A
Quiz 3—C	Quiz 18—D
Quiz 4—D	Quiz 19—C
Quiz 5—C	Quiz 20—C
Quiz 6—C	Quiz 21—C
Quiz 7—B	Quiz 22—D
Quiz 8—A	Quiz 23—B
Quiz 9—D	Quiz 24—D
Quiz 10—B	Quiz 25—A
Quiz 11—B	Quiz 26—D
Quiz 12—D	Quiz 27—D
Quiz 13—D	Quiz 28—D
Quiz 14—B	Quiz 29—A
Quiz 15—A	Quiz 30—B

ANSWERS

LEVEL 7

Quiz 1—A	Quiz 16—A
Quiz 2—D	Quiz 17—B
Quiz 3—B	Quiz 18—B
Quiz 4—D	Quiz 19—B
Quiz 5—C	Quiz 20—B
Quiz 6—B	Quiz 21—B
Quiz 7—A	Quiz 22—B
Quiz 8—C	Quiz 23—C
Quiz 9—A	Quiz 24—A
Quiz 10—A	Quiz 25—A
Quiz 11—D	Quiz 26—B
Quiz 12—D	Quiz 27—D
Quiz 13—A	Quiz 28—C
Quiz 14—B	Quiz 29—A
Quiz 15—A	Quiz 30—B

ANSWERS

SILVER

Quiz 1—A	Quiz 16—B
Quiz 2—B	Quiz 17—C
Quiz 3—A	Quiz 18—C
Quiz 4—C	Quiz 19—D
Quiz 5—A	Quiz 20—B
Quiz 6—D	Quiz 21—D
Quiz 7—B	Quiz 22—B
Quiz 8—A	Quiz 23—A
Quiz 9—B	Quiz 24—A
Quiz 10—C	Quiz 25—D
Quiz 11—B	Quiz 26—C
Quiz 12—C	Quiz 27—A
Quiz 13—D	Quiz 28—A
Quiz 14—C	Quiz 29—B
Quiz 15—C	Quiz 30—D

ANSWERS

LEVEL 9

Quiz 1—A	Quiz 16—D
Quiz 2—D	Quiz 17—B
Quiz 3—B	Quiz 18—C
Quiz 4—C	Quiz 19—B
Quiz 5—C	Quiz 20—B
Quiz 6—D	Quiz 21—B
Quiz 7—A	Quiz 22—D
Quiz 8—A	Quiz 23—D
Quiz 9—B	Quiz 24—C
Quiz 10—D	Quiz 25—B
Quiz 11—B	Quiz 26—A
Quiz 12—A	Quiz 27—C
Quiz 13—D	Quiz 28—B
Quiz 14—D	Quiz 29—C
Quiz 15—B	Quiz 30—B

250

ANSWERS

LEVEL 10

Quiz 1—A
Quiz 2—A
Quiz 3—A
Quiz 4—B
Quiz 5—A
Quiz 6—C
Quiz 7—D
Quiz 8—A
Quiz 9—B
Quiz 10—B
Quiz 11—A
Quiz 12—C
Quiz 13—B
Quiz 14—B
Quiz 15—D

Quiz 16—D
Quiz 17—C
Quiz 18—B
Quiz 19—A
Quiz 20—A
Quiz 21—A
Quiz 22—B
Quiz 23—D
Quiz 24—B
Quiz 25—B
Quiz 26—D
Quiz 27—A
Quiz 28—D
Quiz 29—A
Quiz 30—B

ANSWERS

LEVEL 11

Quiz 1—A	Quiz 16—C
Quiz 2—B	Quiz 17—C
Quiz 3—D	Quiz 18—D
Quiz 4—D	Quiz 19—B
Quiz 5—B	Quiz 20—B
Quiz 6—B	Quiz 21—D
Quiz 7—D	Quiz 22—D
Quiz 8—C	Quiz 23—D
Quiz 9—D	Quiz 24—B
Quiz 10—A	Quiz 25—B
Quiz 11—D	Quiz 26—A
Quiz 12—B	Quiz 27—C
Quiz 13—B	Quiz 28—B
Quiz 14—C	Quiz 29—B
Quiz 15—A	Quiz 30—B

ANSWERS

GOLD

Quiz 1—A

Quiz 2—B

Quiz 3—A

Quiz 4—D

Quiz 5—B

Quiz 6—B

Quiz 7—A

Quiz 8—C

Quiz 9—C

Quiz 10—B

Quiz 11—A

Quiz 12—B

Quiz 13—D

Quiz 14—C

Quiz 15—B

Quiz 16—B

Quiz 17—A

Quiz 18—B

Quiz 19—D

Quiz 20—B

Quiz 21—D

Quiz 22—D

Quiz 23—C

Quiz 24—D

Quiz 25—D

Quiz 26—A

Quiz 27—D

Quiz 28—A

Quiz 29—C

Quiz 30—D